A PRESOCRATICS READER

A PRESOCRATICS READER

Edited, with Introduction, by
PATRICIA CURD

Translations by
RICHARD D. MCKIRAHAN, JR.

HACKETT PUBLISHING COMPANY, INC.
Indianapolis/Cambridge

Previous materials copyright©1995 by
  Hackett Publishing Company, Inc.

New materials copyright©1996 by
  Hackett Publishing Company, Inc.

Printed in the United States of America

01 00   3 4 5 6

For further information, please address

Hackett Publishing Company, Inc.
P.O. Box 44937
Indianapolis, Indiana 46244-0937

Cover design by Listenberger Design & Associates

Text design by Dan Kirklin
Typeset by AeroType, Inc.

Library of Congress Cataloging-in-Publication Data

A Presocratics reader/edited, with introduction, by Patricia Curd;
  translations by Richard D. McKirahan, Jr.
      p.   cm.
  Includes bibliographical references.
    ISBN 0-87220-327-1 (cloth).   ISBN 0-87220-326-3 (pbk.)
    1. Pre-Socratic philosophers.   I. Curd, Patricia, 1949–
  II. McKirahan, Richard D.
  B187.5.P75 1996
  182 – dc20   95-39291
                                                        CIP

CONTENTS*

Preface   vi
References   vii
Maps   viii
Time Line   xi
Acknowledgments   xii

Introduction   1
The Milesians   9
    Thales   9
    Anaximander   11
    Anaximenes   14
Pythagoras and Pythagoreanism   17
    Philolaus   22
Xenophanes   25
Heraclitus   29
Parmenides   43
The Pluralists: Anaxagoras and Empedocles   53
    Anaxagoras   53
    Empedocles   60
Zeno of Elea   73
Atomism: Leucippus and Democritus   79
Melissus   89
Diogenes of Apollonia   93
The Sophists   97
    Protagoras   98
    Gorgias   99
    Antiphon   104
    Critias   107
Suggestions for Further Reading   109
Concordance and Sources   113

*Except where noted, translations are by R. D. McKirahan, Jr.

PREFACE

This volume is a slightly revised and expanded version of the Presocratics and Sophists section of *Readings in Ancient Greek Philosophy* (Hackett Publishing Co., 1995). Like the volume from which it derives, *A Presocratics Reader* offers a selection of the extant remains of early Greek philosophical thought together with unobtrusive editorial material. The selections include cosmology, metaphysics, epistemology, and ethics, but they do not cover the whole range of the rich body of material that we have from the Presocratics and the Sophists. For those who wish to explore Presocratic thought further or who desire more analysis and interpretation, suggestions for further reading are included at the end of the book.

Most of the translations are by Richard D. McKirahan, Jr., and are from his book, *Philosophy Before Socrates* (Hackett Publishing Co., 1994), which is an excellent detailed study of the figures introduced here. In a few places, all of which are noted, I have deviated from his translations. Asterisked notes to the translations are by the translator of that text. S. Marc Cohen and C.D.C. Reeve were exemplary co-editors on *Readings in Ancient Greek Philosophy*, and they offered help and advice on this volume, for which I am very grateful.

REFERENCES

References to the Presocratic philosophers make use of the standard edition of texts, *Die Fragmente der Vorsokratiker*, by H. Diels, revised by W. Kranz (commonly referred to as "DK"). DK assigns a unique number to each philosopher or Sophist, and uses the letter "A" to indicate testimonia written about a Presocratic thinker by someone else, and the letter "B" to indicate fragments of that person's own works. Thus, "22A2" refers to the second of the testimonia about Heraclitus (who is assigned number 22); "28B3" refers to the third fragment of Parmenides (number 28).

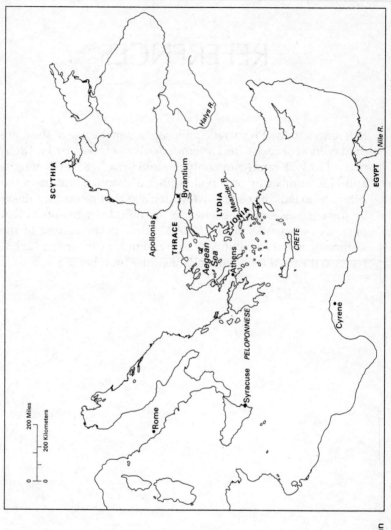

SCYTHIA

Halys R.

Byzantium

Apollonia

THRACE

LYDIA

Meander R.

IONIA

Aegean Sea

Athens

CRETE

Nile R.

EGYPT

Cyrene

PELOPONNESE

Syracuse

Rome

200 Miles

200 Kilometers

0

0

The Eastern
Mediterranean

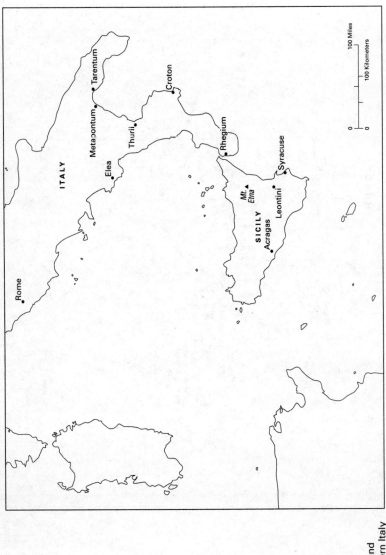

Sicily and
Southern Italy

x

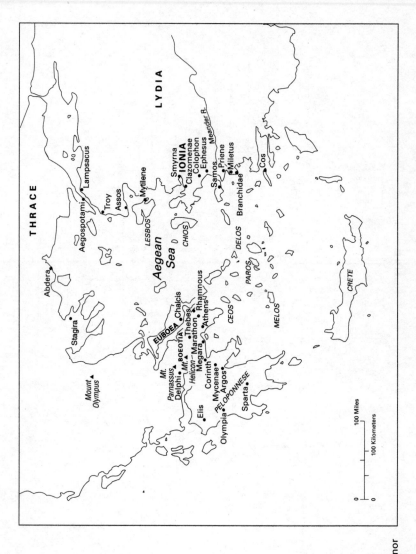

Greece and
Western Asia Minor

TIME LINE

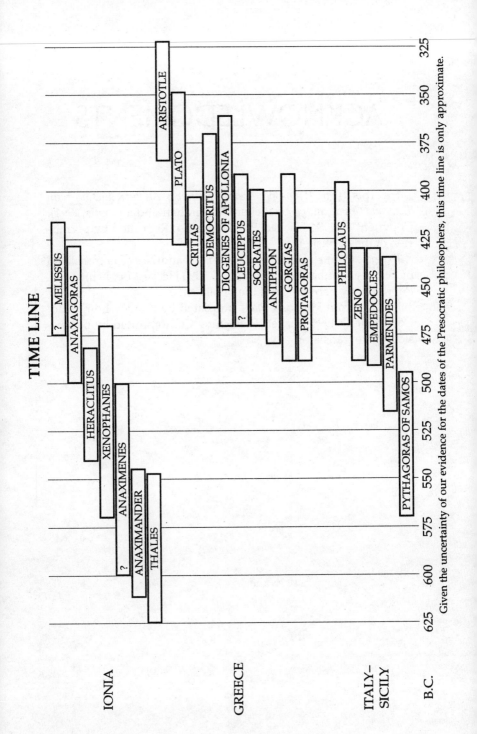

Given the uncertainty of our evidence for the dates of the Presocratic philosophers, this time line is only approximate.

ACKNOWLEDGMENTS

Excerpts from *Philosophy Before Socrates: An Introduction with Texts and Commentary,* by Richard McKirahan (Indianapolis: 1994). Copyright © 1994 Hackett Publishing Co. Reprinted by permission of the publisher.

Excerpt from Hesiod's *Works and Days* and *Theogony* translated by Stanley Lombardo. Copyright © 1993 Hackett Publishing Co. Reprinted by permission of the publisher.

Excerpt from Homer's *Iliad,* translated by Stanley Lombardo. Copyright © 1995 Hackett Publishing Co. Reprinted by permission of the translator.

INTRODUCTION

In 585 B.C. Thales of Miletus reportedly predicted an eclipse of the sun. Although we know none of the details of his prediction, this event has traditionally marked the beginning of philosophy and science in Western thought. Although many people, from Aristotle to modern scholars, have speculated as to why Western philosophy and science began in Miletus, a Greek city on the Ionian coast of Asia Minor, no one really knows the answer. So both the circumstances and the particular event that tradition has chosen for the origin of Western philosophy are shrouded in uncertainty. But uncertain as the details may be, it is clear that Thales stands at the beginning of a great tradition of rational and critical speculation and thought about the world and the place of human beings in it that continues to the present day.

Thales was the first of a succession of thinkers known as the Presocratic philosophers who lived and worked in Greece before and during the lifetime of Socrates (470–399). They do not belong to any unified school of thought, but they share intellectual attitudes and assumptions and a spirit of enthusiastic rational inquiry that makes it reasonable to regard them as a group. It was not simply Thales' prediction of an eclipse that justifies our naming him the first Western philosopher and scientist—after all, both the Egyptians and the Babylonians had complex astronomies. But Thales and his fellow-Milesians Anaximander and Anaximenes manifested an outlook that truly marks the beginning of philosophy. Part of this outlook was a commitment to argument and critical inquiry, together with a view about the nature of justification. Another was the belief that the natural world, indeed the entire universe, could be explained in terms that do not refer to anything beyond nature itself. Thales claimed that everything is really water in some form or other, that water, by undergoing certain natural processes, both becomes and accounts for everything there is. This may strike us as a rather crude and naïve claim.

1

But Aristotle, one of the earliest historians of philosophy, suggests that Thales had reasons for holding it and arguments to back it up:

> Maybe he got this idea from seeing that the nourishment of all things is moist, and that the hot itself comes to be from this and lives on this (the principle of all things is that from which they come to be)—getting this idea from this consideration and also because the seeds of all things have a moist nature; and water is the principle of the nature of moist things. (Aristotle, *Metaphysics* 983b18–27 = DK11A12)

On Aristotle's view, Thales' theory is based on evidence acquired by inquiry and on reasoning about that evidence. We may contrast Thales' account of the character of the natural world with the story of the origin of the cosmos offered by Hesiod (probably in the century before Thales):

> Tell me these things, Olympian Muses,
> From the beginning, and tell which of them came first.
> In the beginning there was only Chaos, the Abyss,
> But then Gaia, the Earth, came into being,
> Her broad bosom the ever-firm foundation of all,
> And Tartaros, dim in the underground depths,
> And Eros, loveliest of all the Immortals, who
> Makes their bodies (and men's bodies) go limp,
> Mastering their minds and subduing their wills.
> From the Abyss were born Erebos and dark Night.
> And Night, pregnant after sweet intercourse
> With Erebos, gave birth to Aether and Day.
> Earth's first child was Ouranos, starry Heaven,
> Just her size, a perfect fit on all sides.
> And a firm foundation for the blessed gods.
> And she bore the Mountains in long ranges, haunted
> By the Nymphs who live in the deep mountain dells.
> Then she gave birth to the barren, raging Sea
> Without any sexual love. But later she slept with
> Ouranos and bore Ocean with its deep currents,
> And also Koios, Krios, Hyperion, Iapetos,
>   Theia, Rheia, Themis, Mnemosyne,
>   Gold-crowned Phoibe and lovely Tethys.

> After them she bore a most terrible child,
> Kronos, her youngest, an arch-deceiver,
> And this boy hated his lecherous father.
>   (Hesiod, *Theogony*, 114–39; tr. Lombardo)

Hesiod invokes the Muses as both the authority for his claims and the source of his information. He does not assume that the story he is about to tell could be deduced from natural evidence, or that he could have arrived at the account of the origins of the universe without supernatural aid, or that he must offer arguments and evidence for his claims. It is enough for him that he has divine warrant for his story. When we turn to the details of the cosmogony (or account of the origins of the universe) we find that it is in fact a theogony (an account of the origins of the gods). Each part of the cosmos is identified with a god who has a distinct personality. The change from Chaos to the presence of Gaia (Earth), Tartaros (the underworld beyond Chaos), Eros (Desire), Erebos (probably the darkness under the earth), and Night is unexplained: Earth and the other gods simply came into being. There is no attempt to explain how or justify that these gods began to exist at just that particular time rather than some other. Once Eros is present, the model of generation is for the most part sexual, though lines 131–32 assert (with no further explanation) that Earth gave birth to the Sea "without any sexual love." These gods, who in some sense are the various parts of the universe, are like humans in their desires and purposes. As in the Egyptian, Sumerian, and Hebrew creation myths, Hesiod makes no clear distinction between a personality and a part of the universe: The natural and the supernatural coincide. And as he feels no compunction about merely asserting his claims without arguments to support them, Hesiod clearly thinks that the proper response to his story is unquestioning acceptance rather than critical scrutiny and rational agreement or disagreement.

The Presocratic philosophers rejected both Hesiod's sort of explanation and his attitude to uncritical belief. But we should be careful not to overstate the case here: In the fragments of Presocratic philosophy we shall find gaps in rational explanation, appeals to the Muses or to divine warrant, and breaks in the connection between theory and evidence. But despite all this, the Presocratic philosophers took a bold leap in adopting this critical attitude. In the case of the three Milesians, for instance, we find each proposing a different thing as the one fundamental reality of the cosmos. Anaximander, who followed Thales, rejected his idea that water is the basic stuff. Perhaps he thought that water was too specific a thing to change into everything else; at any rate, in its place he hypothesized a single material reality that had no specific characteristics, something he called the indefinite (or the boundless). Anaximander's pupil and follower, Anaximenes, in turn rejected his view, apparently arguing that the boundless was too indefinite to do the job Anaximander thought it could. Anaximenes suggested that air is the one basic stuff of the universe. Moreover, he saw that there was a gap in the views of Thales and Anaximander, because they had provided no mechanism for the changes their single stuffs underwent in the process of becoming everything else. Anaximenes remedies this omission by proposing that air becomes everything else by the processes of condensation and rarefaction. From just this brief look at their views, it is clear that, despite their disagreements, the Milesians worked within a shared framework of argument and justification.

In adopting this critical attitude, the Presocratics faced the question of just what a human being could, as a matter of fact, know. The Milesians might give arguments for their claims that everything is really a form of water, or air, but how could they actually justify claims about an original state of the universe that none of them had experienced? Hesiod would have had an answer to this question. As we have seen, he calls on the divine Muses to establish the truth of his claims about the births of the gods. Similarly, in the *Iliad*, we find Homer calling on the Muses to tell him the catalogue of the ships and men who went to Troy. The Muses are divine and immortal: They were there and thus are appropriate both as witnesses to the truth and as assurance that the story Homer tells is true. In Homer and Hesiod we find the same mechanism, the divine warrant of the Muses, invoked to justify different sorts of claims, the one religious and cosmogonical, the other historical.

> Tell me now, Muses,
> Who live on Olympus—for you are
> Goddesses, and are present,
> And know all things, while we

> Hear only reports and know nothing—
> Who were the Greek captains and lords?
> The rank and file I could never name,
> Not even if I had ten tongues, ten mouths,
> A voice that never broke and a bronze heart,
> Unless the Olympian Muses, daughters
> Of Zeus Aegis-holder, called to my mind
> All those who came under Ilion's walls.
>   (*Iliad* 2. 484–92; tr. Lombardo)

But in rejecting divine authority as the warrant for their claims, the Presocratics close off an avenue of justification for their theories. A tantalizing mention of this problem appears in the work of Alcmaeon, who echoes Homer, but is far less optimistic about human knowledge: "Concerning things unseen the gods have clarity, but as far as human beings may judge . . ." (DK24B1; tr. Curd). We do not have the end of the fragment but it is likely that Alcmaeon draws a distinction between the all-encompassing divine understanding and the limited knowledge available to humans. Throughout their work, we find the Presocratics wondering what separates sure and certain knowledge from mere belief, and worrying about the very possibility of such knowledge. Moreover, as more and more competing theories about the cosmos appear, the question of what sort of theory can be justified comes to the fore. Sometimes, as we have seen in the debate among the three Milesians, justification is a question of which theory seems best to fit the evidence. But there is another aspect to justification as well, and that is a meta-theoretical question about what constitutes a genuine theory in the first place, no matter what its content. This issue is raised most strikingly by Parmenides of Elea, and Parmenides' powerful arguments about what can be genuinely thought and said haunt the Presocratic philosophers who come after him. Indeed, echoes of these arguments are heard even in the thought of Plato and Aristotle.

Although we call these Presocratics "philosophers," they were, in fact, active in a tremendous number of fields. They would not have thought of astronomy, physics, practical engineering, and what we would call philosophy as separate disciplines, and they would not have thought that engaging in any of these would have precluded their being active in politics. In a society that was

more oral than literary, in which books were just beginning to be
written and distributed, the Presocratics thought and wrote about
an enormous number of things. In the ancient testimonies about
the Presocratics, we find reports of books (or parts of books) on
physics, ethics, astronomy, epistemology, religion, mathematics,
farming, metaphysics, meteorology, geometry, politics, the mechanisms of sense perception, history, and even painting and travel.
They wrote in poetry and they wrote in prose. They were as
interested in the question of how we ought to live as they were in
the problem of the basic material out of which the physical world
is made. Struggling to make philosophical notions clear in a
language that did not yet have technical philosophical terms, they
used elegant images and awkward analogies, straightforward
arguments and intricate paradoxes. Much of their work has not
survived, and we know of it only through the reports and mentions of later philosophers and historians. Most of what has come
to us has been fragments of their work in natural philosophy,
metaphysics, epistemology, and ethics, and the bulk of the material included here is on those topics.

In the latter part of the fifth century, however, there appeared a
number of thinkers primarily interested in moral and political
questions. These were the Sophists. They were independent,
often itinerant, teachers of wisdom and political skills. They
raised questions about the nature of moral virtue and the best way
for a city to be governed, and they took on paying pupils to whom
they taught their rhetorical skills and their social and political
thought. With the Sophists we come to the end of the Presocratic
period. Most of them were contemporaries of Socrates and Plato,
and indeed, Aristophanes, the great comic poet, presents Socrates
himself as a Sophist in his play *The Clouds*. It is worth noting that
in that play Socrates is represented as having the traditional
Presocratic meteorological and cosmological interests (although
in Plato's dialogues, Socrates denies that these are his concerns),
suggesting that our modern distinction between Presocratic philosophers and Sophists may be too extreme.

In studying the Presocratic philosophers, we find ourselves at
the beginning of a great adventure. The metaphysical, episte-
mological, and ethical problems and puzzles that engaged them
became part of the philosophical project that Plato and Aristotle
inherited and then passed on to other, later, philosophers, includ-

ing ourselves. We may find some of their views strange, even bizarre, and we may find that some of their arguments are difficult to comprehend. But the Presocratics saw and understood the importance and usefulness of rational inquiry and the critical evaluation of arguments and evidence. As we join them in this adventure, we become a part of the intellectual tradition that began with Thales' prediction.

Sources

Not a single Presocratic book has survived intact; what we know of the Presocratics is gathered from quotations or summaries in other philosophical works, so our knowledge is fragmentary. Our evidence for Presocratic thought is of two sorts, direct quotations and summaries or references, called testimonia. The Presocratics were quoted and discussed in many ancient books. Below is a list of our most important sources for Presocratic fragments and testimonia.

Both Plato and Aristotle referred to and occasionally quoted Presocratic thinkers, but care must be used in dealing with fragments from these sources. Both often referred to their predecessors for polemical purposes, and both often presented (not always accurate) summaries of positions rather than quotations.

Among our most valuable sources are the commentaries on Aristotle by the Neoplatonist philosopher Simplicius (sixth century A.D.). In his commentaries Simplicius gives long quotations from a number of important Presocratic thinkers, especially Parmenides, Anaxagoras, and Empedocles. Occasionally, and especially in the case of Parmenides, Simplicius tells us that he is quoting more of a certain text than is necessary to make his point because the work in question has become rare and ought to be preserved. Another commentator on Aristotle, Alexander of Aphrodisias (around 200 A.D.), is another such source.

Theophrastus, Eudemus, and Meno, students and followers of Aristotle, wrote histories of philosophy. (These were part of a project organized by Aristotle.) Theophrastus wrote on the "physical opinions" (physics) of the earlier philosophers, while Eudemus concentrated on astronomy, mathematics, and theology, and Meno on medicine. Unfortunately, these works too are lost and survive only in fragments quoted by later thinkers. But where they are available, they provide important insights into Presocratic thought.

The Roman orator and philosopher Cicero (mid-first century B.C.) included quotations from and references to earlier Presocratic thinkers in his accounts of earlier philosophy.

Clement of Alexandria (second half of the second century A.D.) wrote a work called *Miscellanies,* comparing Greek and Christian thought, in the course of which he often quotes Presocratic writings.

Sextus Empiricus, the skeptical philosopher of the second century A.D., quotes a number of Presocratic texts on sense experience and knowledge.

Plutarch, in the second century A.D., quotes from many of the Presocratics in his moral essays. The evidence from Plutarch is complicated by the fact that there are several works also attributed to Plutarch, but not written by him, that also quote the Presocratics (these are designated as by "pseudo-Plutarch"). John Stobaeus (fifth century A.D.) wrote a book called *Eclogae Physicae (Selections on Natural Philosophy)* in which he, too, quoted many Presocratics. H. Diels argued for an earlier (second century A.D.?), lost common source for the work of pseudo-Plutarch and Stobaeus, which he called the *Placita (Opinions)* by Aetius.

In the late second or early third century A.D. Hippolytus, Bishop of Rome, wrote a book called *Refutation of All Heresies.* There he argues that Christian heresies can be linked to Greek philosophical thought. In the course of this ambitious project, he both gives summaries of Presocratic thought and quotes from a number of Presocratics.

Diogenes Laertius (third century A.D.) wrote a wide-ranging but unreliable *Lives of the Philosophers.* Though it contains lively accounts of the lives and work of the Greek philosophers, it must be used with care because it contains much hearsay and invention.

THE MILESIANS

*Three philosophers from the city of Miletus in Ionia, Thales, Anaximander,
and Anaximenes, make up the Milesian "school." Thales is reported to
have been the teacher of Anaximander, who was, in turn, the teacher of
Anaximenes. The three agree that the cosmos began as a single stuff that
changed to become the universe as we see it today. (This view is called
material monism.) They also concur that this underlying stuff constitutes the real and basic nature of all that makes up the cosmos, and that
the original material has within it its own source of motion and change.*

Thales

*Thales is often included among the Seven Sages of Greece, a traditional
list of wise men. Apollodorus suggests that he was born about 625. (We
should accept this date with caution, as Apollodorus usually calculated
birthdates assuming that a man was forty years old at the time of his
greatest achievement. Thus, Thales' suggested birthdate is arrived at by
assuming that he was forty in 585, the year he reportedly predicted the
eclipse.) Plato and Aristotle tell stories about Thales that testify that
even in ancient times philosophers had a mixed reputation for practicality:*

> Once while Thales was gazing upwards while doing astronomy,
> he fell into a well. A clever and delightful Thracian serving-girl
> is said to have made fun of him, since he was eager to know the
> things in the heavens but failed to notice what was in front of
> him and right next to his feet.
>
> (Plato, *Theaetetus* 174a4–8 = 11A9)

> The story goes that when they found fault with him for his
> poverty, supposing that philosophy is useless, he learned from
> his astronomy that there would be a large crop of olives. Then,
> while it was still winter, he obtained a little money and made
> deposits on all the olive presses both in Miletus and in Chios.

9

Since no one bid against him, he rented them cheaply. When the right time came, suddenly many tried to get the presses all at once, and he rented them out on whatever terms he wished, and so made a great deal of money. In this way he proved that philosophers can easily be wealthy if they desire, but this is not what they are interested in.

(Aristotle, *Politics* 1259a9–18 = 11A10)

Thales argued that the basic stuff of the universe was one thing, water, by which he meant either that everything is really water in one form or another or that everything comes from water. Aristotle, who is the source of these reports, seems unsure about which of these propositions Thales adopted; this tells us that even by Aristotle's time Thales was known only by report rather than by any direct evidence. According to the tradition with which Aristotle was familiar, Thales also said that the earth rests or floats on water (though this may be the result of a confusion about his claim that everything is water).

1. Of those who first pursued philosophy, the majority believed that the only principles of all things are principles in the form of matter. For that of which all existing things are composed and that out of which they originally come into being and that into which they finally perish, the substance persisting but changing in its attributes, this they state is the element and principle of things that are. . . . For there must be one or more than one nature out of which the rest come to be, while it is preserved.   (Aristotle, *Metaphysics* 1.3 983b6–18 = 11A2)

2. However, not all agree about the number and form of such a principle, but Thales, the founder of this kind of philosophy, declares it to be water. (This is why he indicated that the earth rests on water.) Maybe he got this idea from seeing that the nourishment of all things is moist, and that the hot itself comes to be from this and lives on this (the principle of all things is that from which they come to be)—getting this idea from this consideration and also because the seeds of all things have a moist nature; and water is the principle of the nature of moist things.   (Aristotle, *Metaphysics* 1.3 983b18–27 = 11A12)

3. Some say it [the earth] rests on water. This is the oldest account we have inherited, and they report that Thales of Miletus gave it. It rests because it floats like wood or some other such thing (for none of them is by nature such as to rest on air, but on water). As though the same argument did not apply to the water supporting the earth as to the earth itself.

(Aristotle, *On the Heavens* 2.13
294a28–34 = 11a14; tr. Curd)

4. Some declare that it [the soul] is mixed in the whole [universe], and perhaps this is why Thales thought all things are full of gods.   (Aristotle, *On the Soul* 1.5 411a7–8 = 11A22)

5. From what has been related about him, it seems that Thales, too, supposed that the soul was something that produces motion, if indeed he said that the magnet has soul, because it moves iron.

(Aristotle, *On the Soul* 405a19–21 = 11A22; tr. Curd)

Anaximander

Diogenes Laertius says that Anaximander was sixty-four years old in 547/546. This dating agrees with the ancient reports that Anaximander was a student or follower of Thales. He was said to have been the first person to construct a map of the world. Anaximander agrees with Thales that there is one material stuff out of which everything in the cosmos comes, but he disagrees about the nature of this stuff. He seems to have argued that if the originating material is something as definite as water (which, after all, has a particular character of its own), then it cannot really become everything else. He claims that the single original material of the cosmos is something indefinite or boundless (apeiron in Greek). This indefinite stuff is in motion, and, as a result of the motion, something that gives rise to the opposites hot and cold is separated off from it (Anaximander does not say what this something is). The hot takes the form of fire, which is the origin of the sun and the other heavenly bodies. The cold is dark mist, which is transformed into air and earth. Both of these are originally moist, but dry as the result of the heat of fire. Thus, in the first development from the moving, indefinite stuff, Anaximander's theory postulates substantial opposites which act on each other and which are the matter for the sensible world. The reciprocal action of the opposites is the subject of fragment B1, the only direct quotation that we have from Anaximander. In the fragment he stresses that changes in the world are not capricious, and with the mention of injustice and retribution he affirms that there are lawlike forces that guarantee the orderly processes of change between opposites.

6. Of those who declared that the first principle is one, moving and indefinite, Anaximander . . . said that the indefinite was the first principle and element of things that are, and he was the first to introduce this name for the first principle [i.e., he was the first to call the first principle indefinite]. He says that the first principle is neither water nor any other of the things called elements, but some other nature which is indefinite, out of which come to be all the heavens and the worlds in them. The things that are perish into the things out of which they come to be, according to necessity, for they pay penalty and retribution to each other for their injustice in accordance with the ordering of time, as he says in rather poetical language.
(Simplicius, *Commentary on Aristotle's Physics* 24.13–21 = 12B1 + A9)

7. This does not have a first principle, but this seems to be the first principle of the rest, and to contain all things and steer all things, as all declare who do not fashion other causes aside from the infinite . . . and this is divine. For it is deathless and indestructible, as Anaximander says and most of the natural philosophers.   (Aristotle, *Physics* 3.4 203b10–15 = 12A15)

8. He declares that what arose from the eternal and is productive of [or, capable of giving birth to] hot and cold was separated off at the coming to be of this cosmos, and a kind of sphere of flame from this grew around the dark mist about the earth like bark about a tree. When it was broken off and enclosed in certain circles, the sun, moon and stars came to be.
(pseudo-Plutarch, *Miscellanies* 179.2 = 12A10)

9. The earth's shape is curved, round, like a stone column. We walk on one of the surfaces and the other one is set opposite.

The stars come to be as a circle of fire separated off from the fire in the cosmos and enclosed by dark mist. There are vents, certain tube-like passages at which the stars appear. For this reason, eclipses occur when the vents are blocked. The moon appears sometimes waxing sometimes waning as the passages are blocked or opened. The circle of the sun is twenty-seven times <that of the earth> and that of the moon <18 times>, and the sun is highest, and the circles of the fixed stars are lowest.   (Hippolytus, *Refutation* 1.6.3–5 = 12A11)

10. Some, like Anaximander . . . declare that the earth is at rest on account of its similarity. For it is no more fitting for what is established at the center and equally related to the extremes to move up rather than down or sideways. And it is impossible for it to make a move simultaneously in opposite directions. Therefore, it is at rest of necessity.
       (Aristotle, *On the Heavens* 2.13 295b11–16 = 12A26)

11. Anaximander says that the sun is equal to the earth, and the circle where it has its vent and on which it is carried is twenty-seven times the size of the earth.   (Aetius 2.21.1 = 12A21)

12. Anaximander says that the stars are borne by the circles and spheres on which each one goes.   (Aetius 2.16.5 = 12A18)

13. Anaximander says that the first animals were produced in moisture, enclosed in thorny barks. When their age increased they came out onto the drier part, their bark broke off, and they lived a different mode of life for a short time.
       (Aetius 5.19.4 = 12A30)

14. He also declares that in the beginning humans were born from other kinds of animals, since other animals quickly manage on their own, and humans alone require lengthy nursing. For this reason, in the beginning they would not have been preserved if they had been like this.
       (pseudo-Plutarch, *Miscellanies* 179.2 = 12A10)

15. Anaximander . . . believed that there arose from heated water and earth either fish or animals very like fish. In these

humans grew and were kept inside as embryos up to puberty.
Then finally they burst and men and women came forth
already able to nourish themselves.

(Censorinus, *On the Day of Birth* 4.7 = 12A30)

Anaximenes

*Anaximenes was said by ancient sources to be a younger associate or
student of Anaximander. Anaximenes agrees with Thales and Anaximander in adopting material monism, but proposes a different underlying reality, which he calls* aer *(usually translated "air" although* aer *is
more like a dense mist than what we think of as air). Aer is indefinite
enough to produce the other things in the cosmos but it is not as vague
as Anaximander's boundless. Anaximander had left it quite unclear just
what it is that comes from the indefinite that is productive of hot and
cold, and Anaximenes may well have argued that the indefinite was too
nebulous a stuff to do the cosmic job Anaximander intended for it.
Anaximenes says that everything is really just* aer *in some form or
other, but he improves on the theories of Thales and Anaximander by
explicitly including in his account the processes, condensation and rarefaction, by which* aer *is transformed into everything else.*

16. Anaximenes . . . like Anaximander, declares that the under-
    lying nature is one and boundless, but not indeterminate as
    Anaximander held, but definite, saying that it is air. It differs
    in rarity and density according to the substances < it be-
    comes >. Becoming finer it comes to be fire; being condensed
    it comes to be wind, then cloud, and when still further con-
    densed it becomes water, then earth, then stones, and the rest
    come to be out of these. He too makes motion eternal and says
    that change also comes to be through it.

    (Theophrastus, quoted by Simplicius, *Commentary
    on Aristotle's Physics* 24.26–25.1 = 13A5)

17. Just as our soul, being air, holds us together and controls us,
    so do breath and air surround the whole cosmos.

    (Aetius, 1.3.4 = 13B2)

18. Anaximenes . . . said that the principle is unlimited [bound-less] air, out of which come to be things that are coming to be, things that have come to be, and things that will be, and gods and divine things. The rest come to be out of the products of this. The form of air is the following: when it is most even, it is invisible, but it is revealed by the cold and the hot and the wet, and movement. It is always moving, for all the things that undergo change would not change unless it was moving. For when it becomes condensed and finer, it appears different. For when it is dissolved into what is finer, it comes to be fire, and on the other hand air comes to be winds when it becomes condensed. Cloud results from air through felting, and water when this happens to a greater degree. When condensed still more it becomes earth and when it reaches the absolutely densest stage it becomes stones.

(Hippolytus, *Refutation* 1.7.1–3 = 13A7)

19. Anaximenes determined that air is a god and that it comes to be and is without measure, infinite and always in motion.

(Cicero, *On the Nature of the Gods* 1.10.26 = 13A10)

20. Anaximenes stated that clouds occur when the air is further thickened. When it is condensed still more, rain is squeezed out. Hail occurs when the falling water freezes, and snow when some wind is caught up in the moisture.

(Aetius 3.4.1 = 13A17)

21. Or as Anaximenes of old believed, let us leave neither the cold nor the hot in the category of substance, but < hold them to be > common attributes of matter which come as the results of its changes. For he declares that matter which is contracted and condensed is cold, whereas what is fine and "loose" (calling it this way with this very word) is hot. As a result he claimed that it is not said unreasonably that a person releases both hot and cold from his mouth. For the breath becomes cold when compressed and condensed by the lips, and when the mouth is relaxed, the escaping breath becomes warm through the rareness.

(Plutarch, *The Principle of Cold* 7 947F = 13B1)

22. When the air is felted the earth is the first thing to come into being, and it is very flat. This is why it rides on the air, as is reasonable.   (pseudo-Plutarch, *Miscellanies* 3 = 13A6)

23. Anaximenes, Anaxagoras and Democritus say that its flatness is the cause of its staying at rest. For it does not cut the air below, but covers it like a lid, as bodies with flatness apparently do, since these are difficult for winds to move because of their resistance. They say that the earth does this same thing with respect to the air beneath. And the air, lacking sufficient room to move aside, stays at rest in a mass because of the air beneath.   (Aristotle, *On the Heavens* 2.13 294b13–20 = 13A20)

24. Likewise the sun and moon and all other heavenly bodies, which are fiery, are carried upon the air on account of their flatness.   (Hippolytus, *Refutation* 1.7.4 = 13A7)

PYTHAGORAS AND PYTHAGOREANISM

Pythagoras was born on the island of Samos in the eastern Aegean sometime around 570; according to tradition, his father was a gemcutter or engraver. He reportedly traveled in Egypt and Babylonia, leaving Samos around 530 to escape the rule of the tyrant Polycrates. Eventually Pythagoras settled in Croton (in Southern Italy) and founded a community that was philosophical, religious, and political. After about twenty years there was an uprising in Croton and elsewhere against the Pythagorean influence; the Pythagoreans were temporarily driven out and many were killed. Pythagoras himself was said to have taken sanctuary in a temple in Metapontum where he starved to death. Despite these and other setbacks, there continued to be Pythagoreans in Southern Italy (one of them, Archytas of Tarentum, was a friend of Plato). Little is known of the views of Pythagoras himself, except that he had a reputation for great learning (a reputation that would later be mocked by Heraclitus), and that he was probably the originator of the important Pythagorean doctrine of the transmigration of souls (a view ridiculed by Xenophanes). Sometime during Pythagoras' life or soon after his death, his disciples split into two groups, the mathematikoi *and the* akousmatikoi. *The* akousmatikoi *were followers who venerated Pythagoras' teachings on religion and the proper way to live (the word* akousmatikoi *comes from* akousmata, *"things heard"), but had little interest in the philosophical aspects of Pythagoreanism. The* mathematikoi *had a great reputation in the ancient world for philosophical, mathematical, musical, and astronomical knowledge (the word* mathematikoi *comes from* mathema, *"study" or "learning"). These different sorts of knowledge were connected in Pythagorean thought, for the Pythagoreans believed that number was the key to understanding the cosmos. Their original insight was that the numerical ratios of the musical scale indicate that the apparent chaos of sound can be brought into rational, knowable order by the imposition of number. They reasoned that the entire universe is a harmonious arrangement (in Greek,* kosmos) *ordered by, and thus knowable through, number. The*

Pythagoreans rejected Ionian methods, and turned from inquiry into the stuff of the universe to a study of its form. This view of the rational arrangement of the universe can be found in the work of Philolaus, the earliest Pythagorean who left a book. He was born in Croton, probably about 470, and so never knew Pythagoras himself, who died around 494. Philolaus claimed that the cosmos was made up of what he termed limiters and unlimiteds, fitted together in what he called a harmonia *(literally a carpenter's joint; also a musical fitting together or harmony). This* harmonia *is expressible in numerical ratios and is thus, according to Philolaus, knowable. In Philolaus we see the Pythagorean assumptions about number at work, although it is possible that Aristotle's famous report that the Pythagoreans said that everything is number is Aristotle's own interpretation rather than a claim that any of the early Pythagoreans actually made (it is not, for instance, clearly present in the extant fragments of Philolaus).*

1. Once [Pythagoras] passed by as a puppy was being beaten, the story goes, and in pity said these words:
   "Stop, don't beat him, since it is the soul of a man, a friend of mine,
   which I recognized when I heard it crying."
                           (Diogenes Laertius, *Lives of the Philosophers*
                                        8.36 = Xenophanes 21B7)

2. Much learning ["polymathy"] does not teach insight. Otherwise it would have taught Hesiod and Pythagoras and moreover Xenophanes and Hecataeus.
                           (Diogenes Laertius, *Lives of the Philosophers*
                                        9.1 = Heraclitus 22B40)

3. Pythagoras the son of Mnesarchus practiced inquiry more than all other men, and making a selection of these writings constructed his own wisdom, polymathy, evil trickery.
                           (Diogenes Laertius, *Lives of the Philosophers*
                                        8.6 = Heraclitus 22B129)

4. Thus [Pherecydes] excelled in both manhood and reverence and even in death has a delightful life for his soul,

if indeed Pythagoras was truly wise about all things,
he who truly knew and had learned thoroughly the opinions
    of men.
                    (Diogenes Laertius, *Lives of the Philosophers*
                                          1.120 = Ion 36B4)

5. There was a certain man among them who knew very holy
      matters
   who possessed the greatest wealth of mind,
   mastering all sorts of wise deeds.
   For when he reached out with all his mind
   easily he would survey every one of the things that are,
   yea, within ten and even twenty generations of humans.
            (Porphyry, *Life of Pythagoras* 30 = Empedocles 31B129)

6. First he declares that the soul is immortal; then that it changes
   into other kinds of animals; in addition that things that happen
   recur at certain intervals, and nothing is absolutely new; and
   that all things that come to be alive must be thought akin.
   Pythagoras seems to have been the first to introduce these
   opinions into Greece.
                    (Porphyry, *Life of Pythagoras* 19 = 14,8a)

7. Heraclides of Pontus says that Pythagoras said the following
   about himself. Once he had been born Aethalides and was
   believed to be the son of Hermes. When Hermes told him to
   choose whatever he wanted except immortality, he asked to
   retain both alive and dead the memory of what happened to
   him. . . . Afterwards he entered into Euphorbus and was
   wounded by Menelaus. Euphorbus said that once he had been
   born as Aethalides and received the gift from Hermes, and told
   of the migration of his soul and what plants and animals it had
   belonged to and all it had experienced in Hades. When Euphorbus died his soul entered Hermotimus, who, wishing to provide evidence, went to Branchidae, entered the sanctuary of
   Apollo, and showed the shield Menelaus had dedicated. (He
   said that when Menelaus was sailing away from Troy he dedicated the shield to Apollo.) The shield had already rotted away
   and only the ivory facing was preserved. When Hermotimus
   died, it [the soul] became Pyrrhus the Delian fisherman, and

again remembered everything. . . . When Pyrrhus died it became Pythagoras and remembered all that has been said.

(Diogenes Laertius, *Lives of the Philosophers* 8.4–5 = 14,8)

8. There are two kinds of the Italian philosophy called Pythagorean since two types of people practiced it, the *akousmatikoi* and the *mathematikoi*. Of these, the *akousmatikoi* were admitted to be Pythagoreans by the others, but they did not recognize the *mathematikoi*, but claimed that their pursuits were not those of Pythagoras, but of Hippasus. . . . The philosophy of the *akousmatikoi* consists of unproved and unargued *akousmata* to the effect that one must act in appropriate ways, and they also try to preserve all the other sayings of Pythagoras as divine dogma. These people claim to say nothing of their own invention, and say that to make innovations would be wrong. But they suppose that the wisest of their number are those who have got the most *akousmata*.

(Iamblichus, *Life of Pythagoras* 81,82 = 18,2 = 58C4)

9. All the *akousmata* referred to in this way fall under three headings. (a) Some indicate what something is, (b) others indicate what is something in the greatest degree, and (c) others what must or must not be done. (a) The following indicate what something is. What are the Isles of the Blest? Sun and Moon. What is the oracle at Delphi? The tetractys, which is the harmony in which the Sirens sing. (b) Others indicate what is something in the greatest degree. What is most just? To sacrifice. What is the wisest? Number, and second wisest is the person who assigned names to things. What is the wisest thing in our power? Medicine. What is most beautiful? Harmony.

(Iamblichus, *Life of Pythagoras* 82 = 58C4)

10. < Pythagoras ordered his followers > not to pick up < food > which had fallen, to accustom them not to eat self-indulgently or because it fell on the occasion of someone's death . . . not to touch a white rooster, because it is sacred to the Month and is a suppliant. It is a good thing, and is sacred to the Month because it indicates the hours, and white is of the nature of

good, while black is of the nature of evil . . . not to break bread, because friends long ago used to meet over a single loaf just as foreigners still do, and not to divide what brings them together. Others < explain this practice > with reference to the judgment in Hades, others say that it brings cowardice in war, and still others that the whole universe begins from this.
(Aristotle, fr. 195 [Rose], quoted in Diogenes Laertius, *Lives of the Philosophers* 8.34–35 = 58C3)

11. At the same time as these [Leucippus and Democritus] and before them, those called Pythagoreans took hold of mathematics and were the first to advance that study, and being brought up in it, they believed that its principles are the principles of all things that are. Since numbers are naturally first among these, and in numbers they thought they observed many likenesses to things that are and that come to be . . . and since they saw the attributes and ratios of musical scales in numbers, and other things seemed to be made in the likeness of numbers in their entire nature, and numbers seemed to be primary in all nature, they supposed the elements of numbers to be the elements of all things that are.
(Aristotle, *Metaphysics* 1.5 985b23–986a2 = 58B4)

12. The elements of number are the even and the odd, and of these the latter is limited and the former unlimited. The One is composed of both of these (for it is both even and odd) and number springs from the One; and numbers, as I have said, constitute the whole universe.
(Aristotle, *Metaphysics* 1.5 986a17–21 = 58B5)

13. The Pythagoreans similarly posited two principles, but added something peculiar to themselves, not that the limited and the unlimited are distinct natures like fire or earth or something similar, but that the unlimited itself and the One itself are the substance of what they are predicated of. This is why they call number the substance of all things.
(Aristotle, *Metaphysics* 1.5 987a13–19 = 58B8)

14. They say that the unlimited is the even. For when this is surrounded and limited by the odd it provides things with the

quality of unlimitedness. Evidence of this is what happens
with numbers. For when gnomons are placed around the one,
and apart, in the one case the shape is always different, and in
the other it is always one.

(Aristotle, *Physics* 3.4 203a10–15 = 58B28)

15. The tetractys is a certain number, which being composed of
the four first numbers produces the most perfect number, ten.
For one and two and three and four come to be ten. This
number is the first tetractys, and is called the source of ever
flowing nature since according to them the entire cosmos is
organized according to *harmonia*, and *harmonia* is a system of
three concords – the fourth, the fifth, and the octave – and the
proportions of these three concords are found in the afore-
mentioned four numbers.

(Sextus Empiricus, *Against the
Mathematicians* 7.94–95, not in DK)

16. They supposed the elements of numbers to be the elements of
all existing things.

(Aristotle, *Metaphysics* 1.5 986a1–2 = 58B4)

Philolaus
(tr. Curd)

17. Nature in the cosmos was fitted together out of unlimiteds and limiters; both the cosmos as a whole and everything
in it.

(Diogenes Laertius, *Lives of the Philosophers*
8.85 = Philolaus 44B1)

18. It is necessary that the things that are be all either limiters or
unlimiteds, or both limiters and unlimiteds; but they could
not always be unlimiteds only. Since, then, it appears that
they are neither from limiters only nor from unlimiteds only,
it is thus clear that both the cosmos and the things in it were
fitted together from both limiters and unlimiteds. And things
in their activities make this clear. For, some of them, from
limiters, limit; some, from both limiters and unlimiteds, both

limit and do not limit; and others, from unlimiteds, will be clearly unlimited.

(Stobaeus, *Selections* 1.21.7a = 44B2)

19. Concerning nature and harmony it is like this: the being of things which is eternal and nature itself admit of divine and not human knowledge except that it was not possible for any of the things that are and are known by us to come to be, without the existence of the being of the things from which the cosmos was put together, both the limiters and the unlimiteds. And since these principles existed, being neither alike nor of the same kind, it would have been impossible for them to be ordered, if harmony had not come upon them, in whatever way it came to be. Those things that are alike and of the same kind were in no need of harmony, but those that are unlike and not of the same kind, nor of the same speed,* it is necessary that these be linked together by harmony, if they are going to be held in an arrangement *(kosmos)*.

(Stobaeus, *Selections* 1.21.7d = 44B6)

20. The magnitude of the scale [*harmonia*] is the fourth and the fifth. The fifth is greater than the fourth by a tone. For from the highest [string; the lowest in pitch] to the middle [string] is a fourth; from the middle to the lowest [string; the highest in pitch] is a fifth; from the lowest [string] to the third is a fourth; from the third to the highest [string] is a fifth. That which is in the midst of the middle [string] and the third is a tone. The fourth is the ratio 3:4, the fifth is 3:2, and the octave is 2:1. Thus the scale [*harmonia*] is five tones and two semitones, the fifth is three tones and a semitone, and the fourth is two tones and a semitone.   (Stobaeus, *Selections* 1.21.7d = 44B6a)

21. And indeed all things that are known have number. For without this nothing whatever could possibly be thought of or known.   (Stobaeus, *Selections* 1.21.7b = 44B4)

22. Number, indeed, has two kinds peculiar to it, odd and even, and a third mixed from both of them, even-odd. And of

*Following the manuscripts with Burkert and Huffman, though "of the same speed" does not make much sense here.

each kind there are many forms, which each thing itself
shows by signs.   (Stobaeus, *Selections* 1.21.7c = 44B5)

23. The first thing to be fitted together [harmonized], the one in
the middle of the sphere, is called the hearth.
                              (Stobaeus, *Selections* 1.21.8 = 44B7)

XENOPHANES

*Born in Colophon, a city on the west coast of Asia Minor, near Ephesus
and Miletus, Xenophanes was a wandering poet and philosopher. We
know, on his own evidence, that he lived to a great age, but the details of
his life are hazy. He was born about 570 and was said to have left Colophon after it fell to the Medes in 546/545. He refers to Pythagoras and
his doctrine of the transmigration of souls in one fragment, and some of
the ancient reports say that he was a teacher of Parmenides. Xenophanes wrote in verse and concerned himself with religious and
philosophical topics as well as more "poetic" matters (one of his fragments is a poem about how to prepare for a symposium, or drinking
party). But he seems to have been keenly interested in religious issues,
including questions about the nature of the gods, and he explored problems in the nature and possibility of human knowledge. Xenophanes
rejected the traditional Olympian accounts of the gods, such as are
found in Hesiod's* Theogony, *arguing that there is a single, non-
anthropomorphic god who is unmoving, but all-seeing, all-hearing, and
all-thinking and who "shakes all things by the thought of his mind." In a
challenge to human claims to have "sure and certain" knowledge about
anything hidden from perception (we should recall that telescopes or mi-
croscopes were not invented until the seventeenth century A.D.),
Xenophanes draws a sharp distinction between knowledge and belief;
but at the same time he suggests that rational inquiry is the best way to
attain what knowledge we can. The fragments and later accounts of his
views suggest that Xenophanes shared with the Milesians an interest in
natural philosophy, although few scientific fragments remain.*

1. Already there are sixty-seven years
   tossing my thought throughout the land of Greece.
   From my birth there were twenty-five in addition to these,
   if I know how to speak truly about these matters.
   (Diogenes Laertius, *Lives of the Philosophers* 9.18 = 21B8)

25

2. Give us no fights with Titans, no, nor Giants
   nor Centaurs—the forgeries of our fathers—
   nor civil brawls, in which no advantage is.
   But always to be mindful of the gods is good.
   (Athenaeus, *Scholars at Dinner* 11.462c = 21B1.21–24)

3. Homer and Hesiod have ascribed to the gods all deeds
   which among men are a reproach and a disgrace:
   thieving, adultery, and deceiving one another.
   (Sextus Empiricus, *Against the
   Mathematicians* 9.193 = 21B11)

4. Mortals believe that the gods are born
   and have human clothing, voice and form.
   (Clement, *Miscellanies* 5.109 = 21B14)

5. Ethiopians say that their gods are flat-nosed and dark,
   Thracians that theirs are blue-eyed and red-haired.
   (Clement, *Miscellanies* 7.22 = 21B16)

6. If oxen and horses and lions had hands
   and were able to draw with their hands and do the same things
     as men,
   horses would draw the shapes of gods to look like horses
   and oxen to look like oxen, and each would make the
   gods' bodies have the same shape as they themselves had.
   (Clement, *Miscellanies* 5.110 = 21B15)

7. Xenophanes used to say that those who say that the gods are
   born are just as impious as those who say that they die, since in
   both ways it follows that there is a time when the gods do not
   exist.   (Aristotle, *Rhetoric* 2.23 1399b6–9 = 21A12)

8. God is one, greatest among gods and men,
   not at all like mortals in body or thought.
   (Clement, *Miscellanies* 5.109 = 21B23)

9. All of him sees, all of him thinks, all of him hears.
   (Sextus Empiricus, *Against the
   Mathematicians* 9.144 = 21B24)

10. But without effort he shakes all things by the thought of
     his mind.
        (Simplicius, *Commentary on Aristotle's Physics* 23.19 = 21B25)

11. He always remains in the same place, moving not at all,
       nor is it fitting for him to go to different places at different
          times.
        (Simplicius, *Commentary on Aristotle's Physics* 23.10 = 21B26)

12. By no means did the gods reveal all things to mortals from the
       beginning,
     but in time, by searching, they discover better.
                              (Stobaeus, *Selections* 1.8.2 = 21B18)

13. No man has seen nor will anyone know
     the truth about the gods and all the things I speak of.
     For even if a person should in fact say what is absolutely the
          case,
     nevertheless he himself does not know, but belief is fashioned
        over all things [or, in the case of all persons].
                                (Sextus Empiricus, *Against the
                                Mathematicians 7.49.110 = 21B34)

14. Let these things be believed as resembling the truth.
                              (Plutarch, *Table Talk* 9.7.746b = 21B35)

15. She whom they call Iris, this thing too is cloud,
     purple and red and yellow to behold.
                              (Scholium BLT on *Iliad* 11.27 = 21B32)

16. Xenophanes says that the things on boats which shine like
       stars,
     which some call the Dioscuri,
     are little clouds which shine as a result of the motion.
                                (Aetius 2.18.1 = 21A39)

17. Sea is the source of water and the source of wind.
     For not without the great ocean would there come to be
     in clouds the force of wind blowing out from within,

nor the streams of rivers nor the rain water of the upper sky,
but great ocean is the sire of clouds and winds and rivers.

(Geneva Scholium on *Iliad* 21.196 = 21B30)

18. Xenophanes declared that the sea is salty because many mixtures flow together in it. . . . He believes that earth is being
mixed into the sea and over time it is being dissolved by the
moisture, saying that he has the following kinds of proofs,
that sea shells are found in the middle of the earth and in
mountains, and the impressions of a fish and seals have been
found at Syracuse in the quarries, and the impression of a
laurel leaf in the depth of the stone in Paros, and on Malta flat
shapes of all marine life. He says that these things occurred
when all things were covered with mud long ago and the
impressions were dried in the mud. All humans are destroyed
when the earth is carried down into the sea and becomes
mud, and then there is another beginning of coming to be,
and this change occurs in all the world orders.

(Hippolytus, *Refutation* 1.14.5–6 = 21A33)

19. All things that come into being and grow are earth and water.

(Philoponus, *Commentary on Aristotle's
Physics* 1.5.125 = 21B29)

20. If god had not created yellow honey,
they would say that figs are far sweeter.

(Herodian, *On Peculiar Speech* 41.5 = 21B38)

HERACLITUS

According to Diogenes Laertius, Heraclitus of Ephesus was born about 540. He was a member of one of the aristocratic families of Ephesus, but tradition tells us that he turned his back on the political life usually associated with such an upbringing, resigning a hereditary ruling position to his brother. He had a reputation for both misanthropy and obscurity (one of his traditional nicknames was "the Riddler"). The former is probably based on his rude references to a number of historians and other philosophers and the latter on the enigmatic paradoxes he generates in expounding his views. He wrote a single book, of which fragment 1 is apparently the opening. Although he made a number of claims about the nature of the universe, he seems to have been as interested in exploring questions about knowledge and the human condition as in exploring cosmological issues (many of his cosmological views can be traced to Xenophanes). He argued that there was a single divine law of the universe, which he called the logos, which rules and guides the cosmos. (The word logos means, among other things, "account," and "thing said" or "word"; like our notion of giving an account, to give a logos is to give an explanation as well as simply to say something.) Although the logos is an independent, objective truth available to all, Heraclitus claimed that most people do not exercise their abilities to come to understand it, acting instead as if they are asleep and in a private world. He thus attempted to bridge the gap between divine and human knowledge pointed out by Xenophanes and Alcmaeon by claiming that there was a link between the divine logos (the account of what there is) and the souls of human beings. Thus Heraclitus claimed that there is a possibility of acquiring sure and certain knowledge, though he ridiculed the wide interests of his predecessors Hesiod, Pythagoras, Xenophanes, and Hecataeus (an early Ionian writer of history or mythography ca. 500). "Much learning," he said, "does not teach understanding." The simple collection of facts will not result in knowledge; rather, there must be insight into and understanding of the significance of these facts. A fundamental part of this insight is seeing how all that is known consti-

29

*tutes a unity. Heraclitus himself offered signs of this unity in his para-
doxes about the unity of opposites. He insisted that, despite the fact that
there is universal change, there is a single, unchanging, law of the
cosmos—the* logos *which both underlies and governs these changes.
Thus one who understands the* logos *can understand the workings of
the cosmos. The physical sign or manifestation of the* logos *is fire, an element that is always changing, yet always the same.*

1. This logos holds always but humans always prove unable to
   understand it, both before hearing it and when they have first
   heard it. For though all things come to be [or, happen] in
   accordance with this *logos,* humans are like the inexperienced
   when they experience such words and deeds as I set out,
   distinguishing each in accordance with its nature and saying
   how it is. But other people fail to notice what they do when
   awake, just as they forget what they do while asleep.
   (Sextus Empiricus, *Against the Mathematicians* 7.132 = 22B1)

2. For this reason it is necessary to follow what is common. But
   although the *logos* is common, most people live as if they had
   their own private understanding. of logos – Good/bad.
   (Sextus Empiricus, *Against the Mathematicians* 7.133 = 22B2)

3. For many, in fact all that come upon them, do not understand
   such things, nor when they have noticed them do they know
   them, but they seem to themselves < to do so >.
   (Clement, *Miscellanies* 2.8.1 = 22B17)

4. The best renounce all for one thing, the eternal fame of mortals, but the many stuff themselves like cattle.
   (Clement, *Miscellanies* 5.59.4 = 22B29)

5. People are deceived about the knowledge of obvious things,
   like Homer who was wiser than all the Greeks. For children
   who were killing lice deceived him by saying, "All we saw and
   caught we have left behind, but all we neither saw nor caught
   we bring with us."   (Hippolytus, *Refutation* 9.9.5 = 22B56)

6. [Heraclitus judged human opinions to be] children's play-
things.   (Stobaeus, *Selections* 2.1.16 = 22B70)

7. They are at odds with the *logos*, with which above all they are in
continuous contact, and the things they meet every day appear
strange to them.   (Marcus Aurelius, *Meditations* 4.46 = 22B72)

8. Divine things for the most part escape recognition because of
unbelief.   (Plutarch, *Coriolanus* 38 = Clement,
Miscellanies 5.88.4 = 22B86)

9. A fool is excited by every word (*logos*).
(Plutarch, *On Listening to Lectures* 40f–41a = 22B87)

10. Dogs bark at everyone they do not know.
(Plutarch, *Should Old Men Take Part in Politics?* 787c = 22B97)

11. What understanding or intelligence have they? They put their
trust in popular bards and take the mob for their teacher,
unaware that most people are bad, and few are good.
(Proclus, *Commentary on Plato's Alcibiades I*,
p. 117, Westerink = 22B104)

12. Of all those whose accounts (*logoi*) I have heard, no one
reaches the point of recognizing that that which is wise is set
apart from all.   (Stobaeus, *Selections* 3.1.174 = 22B108)

13. Every beast is driven to pasture by blows.
([Aristotle] *On the World* 6.401a10 = 22B11)

14. Much learning ("polymathy") does not teach insight. Otherwise it would have taught Hesiod and Pythagoras, and moreover Xenophanes and Hecataeus.
(Diogenes Laertius, *Lives of the
Philosophers* 9.1 = 22B40)

15. Pythagoras the son of Mnesarchus practiced inquiry more
than all other men, and making a selection of these writings
constructed his own wisdom, polymathy, evil trickery.
(Diogenes Laertius, *Lives of the Philosophers* 8.6 = 22B129)

16. Heraclitus said that Homer deserved to be expelled from the contests and flogged, and Archilochus likewise.
(Diogenes Laertius, *Lives of the Philosophers* 9.1 = 22B42)

17. The knowledge of the most famous persons, which they guard, is but opinion. Justice will convict those who fabricate falsehoods and bear witness to them.
(Clement, *Miscellanies* 5.9.3 = 22B28)

18. [Rebuking some for their unbelief, Heraclitus says,] Knowing neither how to hear nor how to speak.
(Clement, *Miscellanies* 2.24.5 = 22B19)

19. Eyes and ears are bad witnesses to people if they have barbarian souls.
(Sextus Empiricus, *Against the Mathematicians* 7.126 = 22B107)

20. Uncomprehending when they have heard, they are like the deaf. The saying describes them: though present they are absent.
(Clement, *Miscellanies* 5.115.3 = 22B34)

21. One ought not to act and speak like people asleep.
(Marcus Aurelius, *Meditations* 4.46 = 22B73)

22. For the waking there is one common world, but when asleep each person turns away to a private one.
(pseudo-Plutarch, *On Superstition* 166c = 22B89)

23. A man in the night kindles a light for himself when his sight is extinguished; living he touches* the dead when asleep, when awake he touches the sleeper.
(Clement, *Miscellanies* 4.141.2 = 22B26)

24. What we see when awake is death, what we see asleep is sleep.
(Clement, *Miscellanies* 3.21.1 = 22B21)

25. Human nature has no insight, but divine nature has it.
(Origen, *Against Celsus* 6.12 = 22B78)

*The same word in Greek may be translated either as 'kindles' or as 'touches'.

26. A man is called infantile by a divinity as a child is by a man.
    (Origen, *Against Celsus* 6.12 = 22B79)

27. The wise is one alone; it is unwilling and willing to be called
    by the name of Zeus.
    (Clement, *Miscellanies* 5.115.1 = 22B32)

28. Thinking is common to all.
    (Stobaeus, *Selections* 3.1.179 = 22B113)

29. It belongs to all people to know themselves and to think
    rightly.   (Stobaeus, *Selections* 3.5.6 = 22B116)

30. I searched myself.   (Plutarch, *Against Colotes* 1118c = 22B101)

31. Men who are lovers of wisdom must be inquirers into many
    things indeed.   (Clement, *Miscellanies* 5.140.5 = 22B35)

32. All that can be seen, heard, experienced—these are what I
    prefer.   (Hippolytus, *Refutation* 9.9.5 = 22B55)

33. Eyes are more accurate witnesses than ears.
    (Polybius, *Histories* 12.27.1 = 22B101a)

34. If all things were smoke, nostrils would distinguish them.
    (Aristotle, *On the Senses* 5.443a23 = 22B7)

35. Souls smell [i.e., use the sense of smell] in Hades.
    (Plutarch, *On the Face in the Moon* 943e = 22B98)

36. Unless he hopes for the unhoped for, he will not find it, since
    it is not to be hunted out and is impassable.
    (Clement, *Miscellanies* 2.17.4 = 22B18)

37. Those who seek gold dig up much earth but find little.
    (Clement, *Miscellanies* 4.4.2 = 22B22)

38. It is weariness to labor at the same things and < always > to be
    beginning [or, It is weariness to labor for the same < masters >
    and to be ruled].   (Plotinus, *Enneads* 4.8.1 = 22B84b)

39. Nature loves to hide.   (Themistius, *Orations* 5.69b = 22B123)

40. The Lord whose oracle is at Delphi neither speaks nor con-
    ceals, but gives a sign.
                        (Plutarch, *On the Pythian Oracle* 404d = 22B93)

41. Wisdom is one thing, to be skilled in true judgment, how all
    things are steered through all things.
             (Diogenes Laertius, *Lives of the Philosophers* 9.1 = 22B41)

42. Let us not make random conjectures about the greatest
    matters.
            (Diogenes Laertius, *Lives of the Philosophers* 9.73 = 22B47)

43. Right thinking is the greatest excellence, and wisdom is to
    speak the truth and act in accordance with nature, while
    paying attention to it.   (Stobaeus, *Selections* 3.1.178 = 22B112)

44. Listening not to me but to the *logos* it is wise to agree that all
    things are one.   (Hippolytus, *Refutation* 9.9.1 = 22B50)

45. Things taken together are whole and not whole, < something
    which is > being brought together and brought apart, in tune
    and out of tune; out of all things there comes a unity, and out
    of a unity all things.
                        ([Aristotle] *On the World* 5.396b20 = 22B10)

46. They do not understand how, though at variance with itself, it
    agrees with itself. It is a backwards-turning* attunement like
    that of the bow and lyre.
                            (Hippolytus, *Refutation* 9.9.2 = 22B51)

47. An unapparent connection *(harmonia)* is stronger than an
    apparent one.   (Hippolytus, *Refutation* 9.9.5 = 22B54)

48. Those who speak with understanding must rely firmly on
    what is common to all as a city must rely on law [or, its law]
    and much more firmly. For all human laws are nourished by

*Reading *palintropos* here (ed.).

one law, the divine law; for it has as much power as it wishes
and is sufficient for all and is still left over.
(Stobaeus, *Selections* 3.1.179 = 22B114)

49. What is opposed brings together; the finest harmony *(harmonia)* is composed of things at variance, and everything comes
to be in accordance with strife.
(Aristotle, *Nicomachean Ethics* 8.2 1155b4 = 22B8)

50. The sea is the purest and most polluted water: to fishes
drinkable and bringing safety, to humans undrinkable and
destructive.   (Hippolytus, *Refutation* 9.10.5 = 22B61)

51. Pigs rejoice in mud more than pure water.
(Clement, *Miscellanies* 1.2.2 = 22B13)
similar

52. Asses would choose rubbish rather than gold.
(Aristotle, *Nicomachean Ethics* 10.5 1176a7 = 22B9)

53. We would call oxen happy when they find bitter vetch to eat.
(Albertus Magnus, *On Vegetables* 6.401 = 22B4)

54. Pigs wash themselves in mud, birds in dust or ash.
(Columella, *On Agriculture* 8.4.4 = 22B37)

55. The most beautiful of apes is ugly in comparison with the
human race.   (Plato, *Hippias Major* 289a3–4 = 22B82)

56. The wisest of humans will appear as an ape in comparison
with a god in respect of wisdom, beauty, and all other things.
(Plato, *Hippias Major* 289b4–5 = 22B83)

57. The most beautiful arrangement is a pile of things poured out
at random.   (Theophrastus, *Metaphysics* 15
(p. 16 Ross and Fobes) = 22B124)

58. Physicians who cut and burn complain that they receive no
worthy pay, although they do these things.
(Hippolytus, *Refutation* 9.10.3 = 22B58)

59. The track of writing is straight and crooked.*
                    (Hippolytus, *Refutation* 9.10.4 = 22B59)

60. The road up and the road down are one and the same.
                    (Hippolytus, *Refutation* 9.10.4 = 22B60)

61. Upon those who step into the same rivers, different and again
    different waters flow.
                    (Arius Didymus, Fr. 39.2 (*Dox.gr.* 471.4) = 22B12)

62. [It is not possible to step twice into the same river]. . . .
    It scatters and again comes together, and approaches and
    recedes.   (Plutarch, *On the E at Delphi* 392b = 22B91a, b)

63. We step into and we do not step into the same rivers. We are
    and we are not.   (Heraclitus, *Homeric Questions* 24 Oelmann
                    (Schleiermacher, fr. 72) = 22B49a)

64. The beginning and the end are common on the circumference
    of a circle.
                    (Porphyry, *Notes on Homer* (On *Iliad* 24.200) = 22B103)

65. The name of the bow *(bios)* is life *(bios)*, but its work is death.
                    (*Etymologicum Magnum*, sv *bios* = 22B48)

66. Cold things grow hot, a hot thing cold, a moist thing withers,
    a parched thing is wetted.   (John Tzetzes, *Notes on the Iliad*
                    p. 126 Hermann = 22B126)

67. The same thing is both living and dead, and the waking and
    the sleeping, and young and old; for these things transformed
    are those, and those transformed back again are these.
                    (pseudo-Plutarch, *Consolation to Apollonius* 106e = 22B88)

68. Most men's teacher is Hesiod. They are sure he knew most
    things—a man who could not recognize day and night; for
    they are one.   (Hippolytus, *Refutation* 9.10.2 = 22B57)

*Hippolytus has 'gnapheon' ('carding wheels'); sometimes emended to
'grapheon' ('writing') (ed.).

69. They would not have known the name of justice if these things did not exist.   (Clement, *Miscellanies* 4.9.7 = 22B23)

70. Disease makes health pleasant and good, hunger satiety, weariness rest.   (Stobaeus, *Selections* 3.1.178 = 22B111)

71. It is death to souls to become water, death to water to become earth, but from earth comes water and from water soul.
(Clement, *Miscellanies* 6.17.2 = 22B36)

72. The turnings of fire: first, sea; and of sea, half is earth and half fiery waterspout. . . . Earth is poured out as sea, and is measured according to the same ratio (*logos*) it was before it became earth.   (Clement, *Miscellanies* 5.104.3, 5 = 22B31a, b)

73. Fire lives the death of earth and air lives the death of fire, water lives the death of air, earth that of water.
(Maximus of Tyre 41.4 = 22B76a)

74. The cosmos, the same for all, none of the gods nor of humans has made, but it was always and is and shall be: an ever-living fire being kindled in measures and being extinguished in measures.   (Clement, *Miscellanies* 5.103.6 = 22B30)

75. Changing, it rests.
(Plotinus, *Enneads* 4.8.1 = 22B84a; minor rev. Curd)

76. Even the posset separates if it is not being stirred.
(Theophrastus, *On Vertigo* 9 = 22B125)

77. All things are an exchange for fire and fire for all things, as goods for gold and gold for goods.
(Plutarch, *On the E at Delphi* 338d–e = 22B90)
↳ symbollic of what humans

78. Thunderbolt steers all things.   prize
(Hippolytus, *Refutation* 9.10.7 = 22B64)

79. War is the father of all and king of all, and some he shows as gods, others as humans; some he makes slaves, others free.
(Hippolytus, *Refutation* 9.9.4 = 22B53)

80. It is necessary to know that war is common and justice is strife and that all things happen in accordance with strife and necessity. (Origen, *Against Celsus* 6.42 = 22B80)

81. For fire will advance and judge and convict all things. (Hippolytus, *Refutation* 9.10.6 = 22B66)

82. Fire is want and satiety. (Hippolytus, *Refutation* 9.10.7 = 22B65)

83. God is day and night, winter and summer, war and peace, satiety and hunger, but changes the way < fire, > when mingled with perfumes, is named according to the scent of each. (Hippolytus, *Refutation* 9.10.8 = 22B67)

84. It is law, too, to obey the counsel of one. (Clement, *Miscellanies* 5.155.2 = 22B33)

85. To God all things are beautiful and good and just, but humans have supposed some unjust and others just. (Porphyry, *Notes on Homer* (On *Iliad* 4.4) = 22B102)

86. Immortal mortals, mortal immortals [or, immortals are mortal, mortals are immortal], living the death of the others and dying their life. (Hippolytus, *Refutation* 9.10.6 = 22B62)

87. The sun will not overstep his measures; otherwise, the Erinyes, ministers of Justice, will find him out. (Plutarch, *On Exile* 604a = 22B94)

88. The sun is new each day. (Aristotle, *Meteorology* 2.2 355a13 = 22B6)

89. Its [the sun's] breadth is the length of the human foot. (Aetius 2.21 = 22B3)

90. If there were no sun, as far as concerns all the other stars it would be night. (pseudo-Plutarch, *Is Water or Fire the More Useful?* 957a; 22B99)

91. They vainly purify themselves with blood when defiled with it, as if a man who had stepped into mud were to wash it off

with mud. He would be thought mad if anyone noticed him
acting thus.   (Aristocritus, *Theosophia* 68;
                              Origen, *Against Celsus* 7.62 = 22B5)

92. If it were not for Dionysus that they hold processions and
sing hymns to the shameful parts [phalli], it would be a most
shameless act; but Hades and Dionysus are the same, in
whose honor they go mad and celebrate the Bacchic rites.
(Clement, *Protreptic* 34.5 = 22B15)

93. Nightwalkers, Magi, Bacchoi, Lenai, and the initiated.
[These people Heraclitus threatens with what happens after
death. . . .] For the secret rites practiced among humans are
celebrated in an unholy manner.
(Clement, *Protreptic* 22.2 = 22B14)

94. The Sibyl with raving mouth uttering mirthless [and un-
adorned and unperfumed phrases, reaches a thousand years
in her voice on account of the god].
(Plutarch, *Why the Pythia No Longer
Prophesies in Verse* 397a = 22B92)

95. It is death for souls to become wet.   (Numenius, fr. 30;
Porphyry, *The Cave of the Nymphs* 10 = 22B77)

96. A gleam of light is a dry soul, wisest and best.
(Stobaeus, *Selections* 3.5.8 = 22B118)

97. A man when drunk is led by a boy, stumbling and not
knowing where he goes, having his soul moist.
(Stobaeus, *Selections* 3.5.7 = 22B117)

98. Gods and humans honor those slain in war.
(Clement, *Miscellanies* 4.16.1 = 22B24)

99. Greater deaths win greater destinies.
(Clement, *Miscellanies* 4.49.2 = 22B25)

100. Things unexpected and unthought of await humans when
they die.   (Clement, *Miscellanies* 4.22.144 = 22B27)

101. They arise and become vigilant guardians of the living and
     the dead.   (Hippolytus, *Refutation* 9.10.6 = 22B63)

102. How could one fail to be seen by that which does not set?
                               (Clement, *Pedagogue* 2.99.5 = 22B16)

103. Corpses are more fit to be thrown out than dung.
     not homeric   (Plutarch, *Table Talk* 669a = 22B96)

104. You would not discover the limits of the soul although you
     travelled every road: it has so deep a *logos*.
     (Diogenes Laertius, *Lives of the Philosophers* 9.7 = 22B45)

105. The soul has a self-increasing *logos*.
                               (Stobaeus, *Selections* 3.1.180a = 22B115)

106. Every grown man of the Ephesians should hang himself and
     leave the city to the boys; for they banished Hermodorus, the
     best man among them, saying "let no one of us excel, or if he
     does, be it elsewhere and among others."
                               (Strabo 14.25 = 22B121)

107. May wealth never leave you, Ephesians, lest your wicked-
     ness be revealed.   (John Tzetzes, *Scholia on
                                 Aristophanes' Plutus* 88 = 22B125a)
     GAY PRIDE
108. One person is ten thousand to me if he is best.
                               (Theodorus Prodromus, *Letters* 1 = 22B49)

109. A lifetime [or, eternity] is a child playing, playing checkers;
     the kingdom belongs to a child.
                               (Hippolytus, *Refutation* 9.9.4 = 22B52)

110. The people must fight for the law as for the city wall.
                               (Diogenes Laertius, *Lives of the Philosophers* 9.2 = 22B44)

111. Willful violence *(hubris)* must be quenched more than a fire.
                               (Diogenes Laertius, *Lives of the Philosophers* 9.1 = 22B43)

112. A person's character is his divinity.
                               (Stobaeus, *Selections* 4.40.23 = 22B119)

yup - > see earlier note

113. It is not better for humans to get all they want.
                              (Stobaeus, *Selections* 3.1.176 = 22B110)

114. It is better to conceal ignorance.
                              (Plutarch, *Table Talk* 644F. = 22B95)

115. It is difficult to fight against anger, for whatever it wants it
      buys at the price of soul.
                              (Plutarch, *Coriolanus* 22.2 = 22B85)

PARMENIDES

The best reports on the life of Parmenides of Elea suggest that he was born about 515. Diogenes Laertius says that he was a student of Xenophanes "but did not follow him" and that he was also associated at some time in his life with the Pythagoreans although he rejected their theories as well. There is no way of knowing whether or not these reports are true, and it may be that certain similarities between Parmenides' account of being and Xenophanes' account of the single god is the source of the claim about that connection. It is less surprising that Parmenides should have been associated with the Pythagoreans, as Elea is in Southern Italy, home of the Pythagorean movement. Like Xenophanes, Parmenides wrote in verse: His poem is in Homeric hexameters, and there are many Homeric images in it, especially from the Odyssey. In the poem, Parmenides presents himself as being taken in a chariot to meet a goddess, who tells him that he will learn "all things," and assures him that what he is to be told is sure and certain, but adds that he himself must assess the arguments she gives. Parmenides is one of the most controversial figures among the Presocratics, and there is no general agreement among scholars about the details of his theory. In the section of the poem traditionally called Truth, Parmenides argues that genuine thought and knowledge can be only about what is, for what is not is literally unsayable and unthinkable. Parmenides rejects what he calls the "beliefs of mortals" that are based on sense experience and in which there can be "no true trust." Rather, one must judge by understanding what follows from the claim that what-is can be and that what-is-not cannot be or even be thought of. Parmenides proceeds to explore the features of genuine being: What is must be whole, complete, unchanging (it can neither come to be nor pass away, nor can it undergo any qualitative change), and one. Only what has these features can be grasped by the understanding and genuinely known. Given Parmenides' arguments, it becomes clear that the theories of the Milesians, in which a single stuff actually undergoes changes so as to become something else; of Heraclitus, in which opposites are a genuine unity, so that what is both is

and is not; and of the Pythagoreans, where opposites are the basis of
number, are unacceptable to Parmenides. One of the aspects of Parme-
nides' work that is particularly intriguing to modern scholars is that,
having apparently rejected the changing world as literally unreal, he
presents the goddess as giving a cosmological account of the universe—
traditionally called the Doxa *("beliefs" or "opinions")—an account that*
the goddess claims to be deceptive. Is this cosmology supposed to be a
parody of other cosmological accounts? Is it perhaps the best that can be
said for the physical world? Or is the Goddess giving a lesson so that
the hearer who understands both the nature of what-is and the nature of
the deception in the cosmology could give an acceptable cosmological ac-
count? Parmenides' interest in metaphysics and epistemology is
connected with similar interests in Xenophanes and Heraclitus, but Par-
menides was the first Western philosopher to see the importance of meta-
theoretical questions about the nature of philosophical theories, and to
provide comprehensive arguments for his claims. His arguments were
powerful, and his views about knowledge, being, and change became a
serious challenge not only for the Presocratic philosophers who came af-
ter him, but for Plato and Aristotle as well.

1. The mares which carry me as far as my spirit ever aspired
    were escorting me, when they brought me and proceeded
        along the renowned road   *which?*
    of the goddess, which brings a knowing mortal to all
        cities one by one.
    On this path I was being brought, on it wise mares were
        bringing me,
    straining the chariot, and maidens were guiding the way.   5
    The axle in the center of the wheel was shrilling forth the
        bright sound of a musical pipe,
    ablaze, for it was being driven forward by two rounded
    wheels at either end, as the daughters of the Sun
    were hastening to escort < me > after leaving the house
        of Night
    for the light, having pushed back the veils from their
        heads with their hands.   10
    There are the gates of the roads of Night and Day,
    and a lintel and a stone threshold contain them.

High in the sky they are filled by huge doors
of which avenging Justice holds the keys that fit them.
The maidens beguiled her with soft words   15
and skillfully persuaded her to push back the bar for them
quickly from the gates. They made
a gaping gap of the doors when they opened them,
swinging in turn in their sockets the bronze posts
fastened with bolts and rivets. There, straight through
    them then,   20
the maidens held the chariot and horses on the broad
    road.
And the goddess received me kindly, took my
right hand in hers, and addressed me with these words:
Young man, accompanied by immortal charioteers,
who reach my house by the horses which bring you,   25
welcome—since it was not an evil destiny that sent you
    forth to travel
this road (for indeed it is far from the beaten path of
    humans),
but Right and Justice. There is need for you to learn all
    things—
both the unshaken heart of persuasive Truth
and the opinions of mortals, in which there is no true
    reliance.   30
But nevertheless you will learn these too—that the things
    that appear
must genuinely be, being always, indeed, all things.
              (lines 1–30: Sextus Empiricus, *Against the Mathematicians*
        7.111–114; lines 28–32: Simplicius, *Commentary on Aristotle's*
                          On the Heavens, 557.25–558.2 = 28B1)

2. Come now, I will tell you—and bring away my story safely
    when you have heard it—
    the only ways of inquiry there are for thinking:
    the one, that it is and that it is not possible for it not to be,
    is the path of Persuasion (for it attends upon Truth),
    the other, that it is not and that it is necessary for it not
        to be,   5
    this I point out to you to be a path completely unlearnable,

for neither may you know that which is not (for it is not to
   be accomplished)
nor may you declare it.
>   (Proclus, *Commentary on Plato's Timaeus* 1.345.18;
>   lines 3–8. Simplicius, *Commentary on Aristotle's
>   Physics* 116.28 = 28B.2; rev. Curd)

3. . . . For the same thing is for thinking and for being.
>   (Clement, *Miscellanies* 6.23; Plotinus 5.1.8 = 28B3)

4. But gaze upon things which although absent are securely
      present in thought.
   For you will not cut off what is from clinging to what is,
   neither being scattered everywhere in every way in order
   nor being brought together.
>   (Clement, *Miscellanies* 5.15.5 = 28B4; rev. Curd)

5. And it is all common to me
   From where I am to begin; for to there shall I come back again.
>   (Proclus, *Commentary on Plato's Parmenides*
>   1.708 (16 Cousin) = 28B5; tr. Curd)

6. That which is there to be spoken and thought of must be.
   For it is possible for it to be,
   but not possible for nothing to be. I bid you consider this.
   For <I bar> you from this first way of inquiry,
   but next from the way on which mortals, knowing nothing,
   two-headed, wander. For helplessness   5
   in their breasts guides their wandering mind. But they are
      carried on
   equally deaf and blind, amazed, hordes without judgment,
   for whom both to be and not to be are judged the same and
   not the same, and the path of all is backward-turning.
>   (Simplicius, *Commentary on Aristotle's Physics*
>   86.27–28; 117.4–13 = 28B6; slightly rev. Curd)

7. For in no way may this prevail, that things that are not, are.
   But you, bar your thought from this way of inquiry,
   and do not let habit born from much experience compel you
      along this way

to direct your sightless eye and sounding ear and tongue,
but judge by reason the heavily contested testing   5
spoken by me.

    (lines 1–2; Plato, *Sophist* 242a; lines 2–6, Sextus
    Empiricus, *Against the Mathematicians* 7.114 = 28B7)

8. There is still left a single story
  of a way, that it is. On this way there are signs
  exceedingly many—that being ungenerated it is also
    imperishable,
  whole and of a single kind and unshaken and complete.
  Nor was it ever nor will it be, since it is now, all together   5
  one, continuous. For what birth will you seek for it?
  How and from where did it grow? I will not permit you
    to say
  or to think < that it grew > from what is not; for it is not
    to be said or thought
  that it is not. What necessity would have stirred it up
  to grow later rather than earlier, beginning from nothing?   10
  Thus it must either fully be or not.
  Nor will the force of conviction ever permit anything to
    come to be
  from what is not beside it. For this reason, Justice has
    permitted it
  neither to come to be nor to perish, relaxing her shackles,
  but holds fast. But the decision about these matters lies
    in this: 15
  it is or it is not. But it has been decided, as is necessary,
  to let go the one way as unthinkable and nameless (for it
    is not
  a true way) and that the other is and is real.
  How could what is be in the future? How could it come
    to be?
  For if it came into being, it is not, nor if it is ever
    going to be.   20
  In this way, coming to be has been extinguished and
    destruction is unheard of.
  Nor is it divided, since it all is alike;
  nor is it any more in any way, which would keep it from
    holding together,

or any less, but it is all full of what is.
Therefore, it is all continuous, for what is draws near to
    what is.   25
But unchanging in the limits of great bonds,
it is without start or finish, since coming to be and
    destruction
were banished far away and true conviction drove them off.
Remaining the same in the same and by itself it lies
and so stays there fixed; for mighty Necessity   30
holds it in the bonds of a limit, which pens it in all round,
since it is right for what is to be not incomplete;
for it is not lacking; if it were, it would lack everything.
Thinking and the thought that it is are the same.
For not without what is, in which it is expressed,   35
will you find thinking; for nothing else either is or will be
except that which is, since Fate shackled it _tole why_
to be whole and unchanging; wherefore it has been named
    all things
mortals have established, persuaded that they are true—
to come to be and to perish, to be and not < to be >,   40
and to change place and alter bright color.
But since there is a furthest limit, it is complete,
on all sides like the bulk of a well-rounded ball,
evenly balanced in every way from the middle; for it must
    be not at all greater
or smaller here than there.   45
For neither is there what is not—which would
    stop it from reaching
its like—nor is what is in such a way that
    there could be more of what is
here and less there, since it is all inviolate;
for equal to itself on all sides, it meets with its limits
    uniformly.
At this point I stop for you my reliable account and
    thought   50
concerning Truth; from here on, learn mortal opinions,
listening to the deceitful ordering of my words.
For they made up their minds to name two forms,
of which it is not right to name one—in this they have
    gone astray—

and they distinguished things opposite in body, and
   established signs   55
apart from one another—for one, the aetherial fire of flame,
mild, very light, the same as itself in every direction,
but not the same as the other; but that other one, in itself
is opposite—dark night, a dense and heavy body.
I declare to you all the ordering as it appears,   60
so that no mortal opinion may ever overtake you.
       (Simplicius, *Commentary on Aristotle's Physics* 145.1–146.25
       (lines 1–52); 39.1–9 (lines 50–61) = 28B8;
       revised Curd)

9. But since all things have been named light and night
    and the things which accord with their powers have been
       assigned to these things and those,
    all is full of light and obscure night together,
    of both equally, since nothing shares in neither.
       (Simplicius, *Commentary on Aristotle's
       Physics* 180.9–12 = 28B9; rev. Curd)

10. You shall know the nature of the aether and all the signs in
       the aether
    and the destructive deeds of the shining sun's pure
    torch and whence they came to be,
    and you shall learn the wandering deeds of the
       round-faced moon
    and its nature, and you shall know also the surrounding
       heaven,   5
    from what it grew and how Necessity led and shackled it
    to hold the limits of the stars.
       (Clement, *Miscellanies* 5.14, 138.1 = 28B10)

11. . . . how earth and sun and moon
    and the aether which is common to all and the Milky Way and
    furthest Olympus and the hot force of the stars surged forth
    to come to be.   (Simplicius, *Commentary on Aristotle's
       On the Heavens* 559.22–25 = 28B11)

12. For the narrower < wreaths > were filled with
    unmixed fire.

The ones next to them with night, but a due amount of fire is
  inserted among it,
and in the middle of these is the goddess who governs all
  things.
For she rules over hateful birth and union of all things,
sending the female to unite with male and in opposite
  fashion,   5
male to female.

> (Simplicius, *Commentary on Aristotle's Physics*
> 39.14–16 (lines 1–3); 31.13–17 (lines 2–6) = 28B12)

13. First of all gods she contrived Love.

> (Simplicius, *Commentary on*
> *Aristotle's Physics* 39.18 = 28B13)

14. Night-shining foreign light wandering round earth.

> (Plutarch, *Against Colotes* 1116A = 28B14)

15. Always looking towards the rays of the sun.

> (Plutarch, *On the Face in the*
> *Moon* 929AB = 28B15)

16. For as each person has a mixture of much-wandering
      limbs,
   so is thought present to humans. For that which thinks—
   the constitution of the limbs—is the same
   in all humans and every one; for which is more is thought.

> (Theophrastus, *On the Senses* 3 = 28B16)

17. [That the male is conceived in the right part of the
   uterus has been said by others of the ancients.
   For Parmenides says:]
   < The goddess brought > boys < into being > on the right
   < side of the uterus >, girls on the left.

> (Galen, *Commentary on Book VI of Hippocrates'*
> *Epidemics II*, 46 = 28B17)

18. In this way, according to opinion, these things have grown
      and now are
   and afterwards after growing up will come to an end.

And upon them humans have established a name to mark
each one.

(Simplicius, Commentary on Aristotle's On the
Heavens 558.9–11 = 28B19)

19. Such, unchanging, is that for which as a whole the name is
"to be."

(Plato, Theaetetus 180e1 = "The
Cornford Fragment")

THE PLURALISTS:
ANAXAGORAS AND
EMPEDOCLES

The problem faced by subsequent Presocratic philosophers was to find a way to reconcile Parmenides' rejection of change with the possibility of giving a rational account of the changing world of sense experience. Both of the pluralists, Anaxagoras and Empedocles, responded to Parmenides by claiming that the basic substances of the cosmos are entities that have the features of genuine being that he had argued for. Although these entities are eternally real and unchanging, they can be mixed with and separated from each other.

Anaxagoras

Anaxagoras was from Clazomenae, in Ionia. Thus, it is not surprising that he shares with the other Ionian Presocratics an interest in the cosmos. But in Anaxagoras this interest is tempered by an awareness of the metaphysical implications of the work of Parmenides. Anaxagoras was born around 500. He lived for about thirty years in Athens, where he was an associate of Pericles, the famous Athenian politician. He is said to have predicted the fall of a meteorite at Aegospotami in 467, and he said that the sun was a fiery stone rather than a god. His political association with Pericles combined with his nonconformist scientific views resulted in his being prosecuted for impiety (a charge the Athenians would later make against both Socrates and Aristotle). The prosecution took place around 450 (although some reports place the date closer to 430); Anaxagoras was convicted and exiled from Athens to the northern Ionian city of Lampascus (near Troy), where he died in 428. *

---

*Although we can be fairly certain about the dates of Anaxagoras' birth and death, it is not clear just when his philosophical work became available, and it is very difficult to fix the chronological relations among Anaxagoras, Empedocles, and Zeno. Good evidence suggests that Anaxagoras wrote

Anaxagoras envisions an original state for the cosmos in which, as he
says, "All things were together." All things, that is, except Mind
(nous). Mind is said to know and to control all things. At some time,
which Mind chooses, it sets the original mixture into a rotation, as a re-
sult of which things are separated out and recombine with one another
to produce the world we perceive through our senses. The exact details
of Anaxagoras' theory are uncertain, and there is much debate among
scholars as to the correct interpretation of the fragments we have been
left. By "all things" does he mean that everything in the natural world is
already in the mixture? Or is "things" a technical term for Anaxagoras
that includes only the opposites which separate and combine to produce
everything else? Anaxagoras mentions that there are seeds in the origi-
nal mixture. What are we to make of this? Are they elementary particles
of everything, or are they simply biological seeds? There is no agreement
among commentators on these points, but it is agreed that Anaxagoras'
theory is an attempt to continue the Ionian tradition of cosmology in
the face of the enormous challenges of Parmenides' strictures on such
theories.

1. All things were together, unlimited in both amount and smallness. For the small too was unlimited. And when (or, since) all
   things were together, nothing was manifest on account of
   smallness. For air and aither dominated all things, both being
   unlimited. For these are the largest ingredients in the totality,
   both in amount and in size.

   (Simplicius, *Commentary on Aristotle's Physics*
   155.26–30 = 59B1)

2. For both air and aither are being separated off from the
   surrounding multitude and what surrounds is unlimited in
   amount.

   (Simplicius, *Commentary on Aristotle's Physics*
   155.31–156.1 = 59B2)

---

before Empedocles and that Zeno responded to both, and this is the
chronology adopted here; but this is a point that is disputed among
scholars, and there is some evidence for a different ordering of the three.

3. For of the small there is no smallest, but always a smaller (for what is cannot not be). But also of the large there is always a larger, and it is equal in amount to the small. But in relation to itself, each is both large and small.

(Simplicius, *Commentary on Aristotle's Physics* 164.17–20 = 59B3)

4. These things being so, it is necessary to suppose that in all things that are being mixed together there are many things of all kinds, and seeds of all things, having all kinds of shapes and colors and flavors; and that humans too were compounded and all the other animals that possess life; and that there are inhabited cities and cultivated fields for the humans just as with us, and that there are for them a sun and a moon and the rest just as with us, and that the earth grows many things of all kinds for them, of which they gather the most useful into their dwelling and use it. I have said these things about the separating off, because [or, that] it would have occurred not only with us, but elsewhere too.

(Simplicius, *Commentary on Aristotle's Physics* 34.29–35.9 = 59B4a)

5. But before these things separated off, when [or, since] all things were together, not even any color was manifest, for the mixture of all things prevented it—the wet and the dry, the hot and the cold, the bright and the dark, there being also much earth in the mixture and seeds unlimited in amount, in no way like one another. For none of the other things are alike either, the one to the other. Since this is so, it is necessary to suppose that all things were in the whole.

(Simplicius, *Commentary on Aristotle's Physics* 34.21–26 = 59B4b)

6. It is necessary to know that although [or since] these things have been separated apart in this way, all things are not at all less or more (for it is not to be accomplished that they are more than all), but all things are always equal.

(Simplicius, *Commentary on Aristotle's Physics* 156.10–12 = 59B5)

7. And since the portions of both the large and the small are
   equal in amount, in this way too all things would be in
   everything; nor can they be separate, but all things have a
   portion of everything. Since there cannot be a smallest, nothing can be separated or come to be by itself, but as in the
   beginning now too all things are together. But in all things
   there are many things, equal in amount, both in the larger and
   the smaller of the things being separated off.

   (Simplicius, *Commentary on Aristotle's Physics*
   164.26–165.1 = 59B6)

8. . . . and so we do not know either in word or in deed the
   amount of the things being separated off.

   (Simplicius, *Commentary on Aristotle's On the Heavens*
   608.26 = 59B7)

9. The things in the single *cosmos* are not separate from one
   another, nor are they split apart with an axe, either the hot
   from the cold or the cold from the hot.

   (Simplicius, *Commentary on Aristotle's Physics*
   175.12–14; 176.29 = 59B8)

10. As these things are thus rotating and being separated off by
    both force and speed, the speed causes the force, and their
    speed is like the speed of nothing now found among humans,
    but altogether many times as fast.

    (Simplicius, *Commentary on Aristotle's Physics*
    35.14–18 = 59B9)

11. For how could hair come to be from not hair or flesh from not
    flesh?

    (*Scholium on Gregory of Nazianzus* 36.911 Migne = 59B10)

12. In everything there is a portion of everything except Mind,
    but Mind is in some things too.

    (Simplicius, *Commentary on Aristotle's Physics*
    164.23–24 = 59B11)

13. The rest have a portion of everything, but Mind is unlimited
    and self-ruled and is mixed with no thing, but is alone and by

itself. For if it were not by itself but were mixed with something else, it would have a share of all things, if it were mixed with anything. For in everything there is a portion of everything, as I have said before. And the things mixed together with it would hinder it so that it would rule no thing in the same way as it does being alone and by itself. For it is the finest of all things and the purest, and it has all judgment about everything and the greatest power. And Mind rules all things that possess life—both the larger and the smaller. And Mind ruled the entire rotation, so that it rotated in the beginning. And at first it began to rotate from a small area, but it < now > rotates over a greater range and it will rotate over a < still > greater one. And Mind knew all the things that are being mixed together and separated off and separated apart. And Mind set in order all things, whatever kinds of things were to be—whatever were and all that are now and whatever will be—and also this rotation in which are now rotating the stars and the sun and the moon, and the air and aither that are being separated off. This rotation caused the separating off. And the dense is being separated off from the rare and the hot from the cold and the bright from the dark and the dry from the wet. But there are many portions of many things. And nothing is being completely separated off or separated apart one from another except Mind. All Mind is alike, both the larger and the smaller. But nothing else is like anything else, but each single thing is and was most plainly those things of which it contains most.

> (Simplicius, *Commentary on Aristotle's Physics* 164.24–25;
> 156.13–157.4 = 59B12)

14. And when Mind began to cause motion, separating off proceeded to occur from all that was moved, and all that Mind moved was separated apart, and as things were being moved and separated apart, the rotation caused much more separating apart to occur.

> (Simplicius, *Commentary on Aristotle's Physics*
> 300.31–301.1 = 59B13)

15. Mind, which is always, is very much even now where all other things are too, in the surrounding multitude and in things

that have come together in the process of separating and in things that have separated off.

(Simplicius, *Commentary on Aristotle's Physics* 157.7–9 = 59B14)

16. The dense and the wet and the cold and the dark came together here, where the earth is now, but the rare and the hot and the dry went out into the far reaches of the aither.

(Simplicius, *Commentary on Aristotle's Physics* 179.3–6 = 59B15)

17. From these things as they are being separated off, earth is being compounded; for water is being separated off out of the clouds, earth out of water, and out of the earth stones are being compounded by the cold, and these [i.e., stones] move further out than the water.

(Simplicius, *Commentary on Aristotle's Physics* 179.8–10; 155.21–23 = 59B16)

18. The Greeks are wrong to accept coming to be and perishing, for no thing comes to be, nor does it perish, but they are mixed together from things that are and they are separated apart. And so they would be correct to call coming to be being mixed together, and perishing being separated apart.

(Simplicius, *Commentary on Aristotle's Physics* 163.20–24 = 59B17)

19. The sun puts the shine in the moon.

(Plutarch, *On the Face in the Moon* 16 (929b) = 59B18)

20. We call Iris [rainbow] the brightness in the clouds opposite the sun.   (*Scholium BT on Iliad* 17.547 = 59B19)

21. On account of their [the senses'] feebleness we are unable to discern the truth.

(Sextus Empiricus, *Against the Mathematicians* 7.90 = 59B21)

22. Appearances are a sight of the unseen.

(Sextus Empiricus, *Against the Mathematicians* 7.140 = 59B21a)

23. [We are less fortunate than animals in all these respects] but we make use of our own experience and wisdom and memory

and skill, and we take honey, milk < cows >, and laying hold
< of animals > we carry them and lead < them >.

(Plutarch, *On Fortune* 98F = 59B21b)

24. The white of the egg is bird's milk.

(Athenaeus, *Deipnosophists* II 57b = 59B22)

25. [Empedocles and Anaxagoras say that] other things come to
be from the mixture by separation. They differ from one
another in that the former makes a cycle of these separations
and the latter [supposes that there is] only one. Anaxagoras
makes [the principles] infinite, both the uniform parts and the
opposites, but [Empedocles] makes them only the so-called
elements. It seems that Anaxagoras thought the principles
were infinite because he accepted as true the common opinion
of the physicists that nothing comes to be from not being (for
it was on account of this that they say "all things were together," and the coming to be of such and such a thing is
construed as alteration, though some say it is mixture and
separation). [They thought this] also because the opposites
come to be from one another; they must then have been
present in each other. For if everything that comes to be
necessarily comes to be either from being or from not being,
and it is impossible that it come to be from not being (for all
the physicists agree in this belief), they thought that the
alternative followed necessarily, that things come to be out of
things that are, that is, out of things in which they are already
present, but they are imperceptible to us on account of the
smallness of their bulk. On account of this they say that
everything has been mixed in everything, because they saw
everything coming to be from everything. But things appear
to differ from each other and are called by different names
from one another based on what is most predominant in
extent in the mixture of the infinitely many [components].
Nothing is purely or as a whole pale or dark or sweet or flesh
or bone, but whatever each contains the most of is thought to
be nature of that thing.

(*Physics* 1.4 187a23–b6; lines a26–30 = 59A52; tr. Curd)

26. Anaxagoras says the opposite of Empedocles about the elements. For he [Empedocles] says that fire and earth and the others like them are the elements of bodies and everything else is composed of them; but Anaxagoras says the opposite. For the homoiomerous things (I mean flesh and bone and each of the things of that sort) are elements, but air and fire are mixtures of these and of all the other seeds, for each of them is a conglomeration of invisible [amounts] of all the homoiomerous things.

(Aristotle, *On the Heavens* 3.3 302a28–b3; tr. Curd)

27. Anaxagoras . . . says that the elements are unlimited in number. For he makes the elements homoiomerous things, such as bone and flesh and marrow, and each of the others whose parts have the same name [as the whole].

(Aristotle, *On Generation and Corruption* 1.1 314a18–20 = 59A4; tr. Curd)

Empedocles

Born in Acragas, in Sicily, about 492, Empedocles also belongs to the generation of philosophers following Parmenides. He is known to have visited the Southern Italian mainland, and, while he was heavily influenced by Parmenides, there are also traces of Pythagoreanism, the other great philosophical movement of Southern Italy, in his work. At home in Acragas he was an active politician, supporting democracy against oligarchy, even though his aristocratic family connections might have made that support surprising. Empedocles was both a philosopher and a medical man, and he was a truly flamboyant figure. He dressed ostentatiously (ancient reports tell of rich purple robes, a golden diadem, and bronze shoes), claimed magical powers for himself, and in fragment B112 says of himself, "I go about among you, an immortal god, no longer mortal, honored among all, as it seems, wreathed with headbands and blooming garlands." There are many stories of his fantastic activities: Reportedly he kept alive for a month a woman who had no pulse and was not breathing. He diverted two streams to rid the city of Selinus of a plague (and was said to have been acknowledged as a god as a result). Empedocles was exiled from his home and probably died in the Pelopon-

nese, although given his character, it is not surprising that more excit-
ing tales of his death were told. One appears in Diogenes Laertius:
Desiring to show that he was indeed a god, he leapt into the crater of
Mt. Etna. Although the details of his life present the picture of a flashy
and eccentric figure, we should not lose sight of the fact that he constructed a serious and complicated theory of the cosmos and our
knowledge of it, and that he was profoundly interested in the question of
the proper place of human beings in the universe. Like Parmenides, he
wrote in verse, and his poem is addressed to a man called Pausanius,
who was said to have been his lover. He tells Pausanius of the nature of
the cosmos, and of an orginal pure state from which humans have fallen
and to which they may return through a process of purification; like the
Pythagoreans, he argues for a purified life and for vegetarianism. Empedocles argues that there are six basic entities: Earth, Water, Air, and
Fire (later called "elements" by Aristotle) and Love and Strife (Empedocles' two motive forces). Each of these is a genuine being in the
Parmenidean sense. The actions of Love and Strife result in great cosmic
cycles (how many is open to debate), in which Earth, Air, Fire, and Water are mixed together by Love and pulled apart by Strife; the mixture
and separation resemble coming to be and passing away but do not,
for Empedocles, count as the genuine sorts of changes that would be
ruled out by Parmenidean arguments. This mixture and separation results in the world as we perceive it, and Empedocles even gives "recipes"
for the proportion of Earth, Air, Fire, and Water in bone and blood. The
metaphysical dependence of the objects of the sensible world on the four
elements means that the sensible world too is subject to rational explanation and can be known.

28. Friends who dwell in the great city on the yellow Acragas
     on the heights of the citadel, you whose care is good deeds,
     respectful havens for strangers, untouched by evil,
     hail! I go about among you, an immortal god, no
          longer mortal,
     honored among all, as it seems,   5
     wreathed with headbands and blooming garlands.
     Wherever I go to their flourishing cities,
     I am revered by the men and women. And they
          follow together

in tens of thousands, inquiring where lies the path to
    profit,
some in need of prophecy, while others,   10
pierced for a long time with harsh pains,
asked to hear the voice of healing for all diseases.
    (Diogenes Laertius, *Lives of the Philosophers* 8.62 (lines 1–10);
            Clement, *Miscellanies* 6.30 (lines 9–11) = 31B112)

29. If you fix them in your strong intelligence
    and gaze upon them propitiously with pure attention,
    these things will all be very much present to you all your
        life long
    and from them you will obtain many others. For these very
        things
    grow into each kind of character, depending on each
        person's nature.   5
    But if you reach out for other kinds of things, the millions
    of evils that are found among men which blunt their
        thoughts,
    indeed they will leave you immediately as time revolves,
    longing to come to their own dear kind.
    For know that all things possess thought and a portion of
        intelligence.   10
                    (Hippolytus, *Refutation* 7.29.25 = 31B110)

30. But come, I shall first tell you the beginning . . .
    from which all that we now look upon came to be clear,
    earth and the sea with many waves and moist air
    and the Titan aither, squeezing all things round about in
        a circle.   (Clement, *Miscellanies* 5.48.3 = 31B38)

31. It is not possible to reach and approach [the divine] with
        the eyes
    or grasp < it > with our hands, by which the most powerful
    highway of persuasion strikes the minds of men.
                        (Clement, *Miscellanies* 5.81.2 = 31B133)

32. I will tell a double story. For at one time they grow to be
        only one

out of many, but at another they grow apart to be many
    out of one.
Double is the coming to be of mortal things, and double is
    their failing.
For the coming together of all things produces one birth
    and destruction,
and the other is nurtured and flies apart when they grow
    apart again.   5
And these never cease continually interchanging,
at one time all coming together into one by Love
and at another each being borne apart by the hatred of
    Strife.
Thus in that they have learned to grow to be one out of
    many
and in that they again spring apart as many when the one
    grows apart,   10
in that way they come to be and their life is not lasting,
but in that they never cease interchanging continually,
in this way they are always unchanging in a cycle.
But come, listen to my words, for learning increases
    wisdom.
For as I previously said, while declaring the bounds of
    my words,   15
I will tell a double story. For at one time they grew to be
    only one
out of many, but at another they grew apart to be many
    out of one:
fire and water and earth and the immense height of air,
and deadly Strife apart from them, equal in all
    directions
and Love among them, equal in length and breadth.   20
Behold her with your mind, and do not sit with your eyes
    staring in amazement.
She is also recognized as innate in mortal limbs.
Through her they have kindly thoughts and do peaceful
    deeds,
calling her by the appellation Joy and also Aphrodite.
No mortal man has seen her spinning   25
among them. But listen to the undeceitful course of my
    account.

For these [the four elements] are all equal and of the same
   age,
but each rules in its own province and possesses its own
   individual character,
but they dominate in turn as time revolves.
And nothing is added to them, nor do they leave off,   30
for if they were perishing continuously, they would no
   longer be.
But what could increase this totality? And where would it
   come from?
And how [or, where] could it perish, since nothing is empty
   of these?
But there are just these very things, and running through
   one another
at different times they come to be different things and
   yet are always and continuously the same.   35
            (Simplicius, *Commentary on Aristotle's Physics*
                              158.1–159.4 = 31B17)

33. Hear first the four roots of all things:
    Shining Zeus and life-bringing Hera and Aidoneus
    and Nestis who with her tears moistens mortal Springs.
                         (Aetius 1.3.20 = 31B6)

34. But come, behold this witness of my previous discourse,
    if anything in the foregoing was feeble in form:
    the sun, brilliant to see and hot everywhere,
    all the immortal things that are drenched in the heat and
       shining light,
    and rain in all things, dark and cold,   5
    and from earth stream forth things rooted and solid.
    In Anger they are all separate and have their own forms,
    but they come together in Love and yearn for one another.
    For from these come all things that were and are and will
       be in the future.
    Trees have sprouted and men and women,
    and beasts and birds and fishes nurtured in water,
    and long-lived gods highest in honors.
    For there are just these things, and running through one
       another

they come to have different appearances, for mixture changes
them.   (Simplicius, *Commentary on Aristotle's Physics*
159.13–26 = 31B21)

35. For they are as they have been previously* and will be, and
never, I think,
will endless time be empty of both of these [i.e., Strife
and Love].   (Hippolytus, *Refutation* 7.29.9 = 31B16)

36. As when painters decorate votive offerings—
men through cunning well taught in their skill—
who when they take the many colored pigments in their
hands,
mixing in harmony more of these and less of those,
out of them they produce shapes similar to all things,   5
creating trees and men and women
and beasts and birds and fishes nurtured in water
and long-lived gods highest in honors.
So let not deception compel your mind to believe that
there is from anywhere else
a source of mortal things, all the endless numbers of   10
things which have come to be manifest,
but know these things distinctly, having heard the story
from a god.
(Simplicius, *Commentary on Aristotle's Physics*
160.1–11 = 31B23)

37. As then Cypris, busily working on shapes [or, kinds of
things] moistened earth in rain,
and gave it to swift fire to strengthen . . .
(Simplicius, *Commentary on Aristotle's On the
Heavens* 530.6–7 = 31B73)

38. . . . all of them that are dense within, while their exterior
parts are formed in a loose texture,
because they met with such moisture in the hands of Cypris.
(Simplicius, *Commentary on Aristotle's On the
Heavens* 530.9–10 = 31B75)

*Reading *Esti gar hōs paros ēn* (Lloyd-Jones).

39. < Water > has a greater affinity with wine, but with olive oil
    it is unwilling < to mix >.
    (Philoponus, *Commentary on Aristotle's Generation
    of Animals* 123.19–20 = 31B91)

40. [On the question why mules are sterile, Empedocles explains
    that the mixture of seeds becomes thick, although the seed of
    both the horse and the ass is soft. For the hollow parts of each
    fit together with the thick parts of the other, and as a result a
    hard substance comes from soft ones] like copper mixed with
    tin.   (Aristotle, *Generation of Animals* 747a34–67 = 31B92)

41. Pleasant earth in her well-made crucibles obtained
    two parts of bright Nestis out of the eight,
    and four of Hephaestus, and white bones came into being,
    fitted together divinely by the glues of Harmonia.
    (Simplicius, *Commentary on Aristotle's Physics*
    300.21–24 = 31B96)

42. Earth came together by chance in about equal quantity
        to these,
    Hephaestus and rain and all-shining aither,
    anchored in the perfect harbors of Cypris,
    either a bit more or a bit less of it among more of them.
    From them blood came into being and other forms of flesh. 5
    (Simplicius, *Commentary on Aristotle's Physics*
    32.6–10 = 31B98)

43. Fools. For their thoughts are not far-reaching,
    who expect that there comes to be what previously was not,
    or that anything perishes and is completely destroyed.
    (Plutarch, *Against Colotes* 1113c = 31B11)

44. For it is impossible to come to be from what in no way is,
    and it is not to be accomplished and is unheard of that what
        is perishes absolutely.
    For each time it will be where a person thrusts it each time.
    ([Aristotle] *On Melissus Xenophanes Gorgias*
    975b1–4 = 31B12)

45. I will tell you another thing. There is coming to be of not a
     single one of all
     mortal things, nor is there any end of deadly death,
     but only mixture, and separation of what is mixed,
     and nature is the name given to them by humans.
                         (Plutarch, *Against Colotes* 1111F = 31B8)

46. Whenever they arrive in the aither mixed so as to
     form a man
     or one of the wild beasts or bushes
     or birds, that is when <people> speak of coming into being;
     and whenever they are separated, that < is what they call> the
     ill-starred fate of death.
     They do not call it as is right, but I myself too assent to their
     convention.   (Plutarch, *Against Colotes* 1113D = 31B9)

47. None of the whole is either empty or over-full.
                         (Aetius 1.18.2 = 31B13)

48. But I shall return to that path of songs
     which I recounted before, drawing off from one account
        this account.
     When Strife had reached the lowest depth
     of the vortex, and Love comes to be in the middle of the
        whirl,
     at this point all these things come together to be one
        single thing,   5
     not at once, but willingly banding together, different ones
        from different places.
     As they were mixed, myriads of tribes of mortal things
        poured forth,
     but many contrariwise remained unmixed while they were
        mingling—
     all that Strife still held back aloft. For it had not
     entirely completed its blameless retreat from them to the
        furthest limits of the circle,   10
     but it remained in some of the limbs, while from others
        it had withdrawn.
     But as far as it would continually run out ahead, so far
        continually would follow in pursuit

the gentle immortal onset of blameless Love.
Immediately things became mortal which formerly had
    learned to be immortal,
and things previously unmixed became mixed,
    interchanging their paths.   15
As they were mixed, myriads of tribes of mortal things
    poured forth,
fitted with all kinds of forms, a wonder to behold.
                (Simplicius, *Commentary on Aristotle's On the Heavens*
                        529.1–15 (lines 1–15); *Commentary on Aristotle's*
                                Physics 32.13–33.2 (lines 3–17) = 31B35)

49. When they were coming together, Strife was being
    displaced to the extremity.
                        (Stobaeus, *Selections* 1.10.11 = 31B36)

50. They [i.e., the four elements] dominate in turn as the cycle
        revolves,
    and they decrease into one another and grow in their turn,
        as destined.
    For there are just these things, and running through one
        another
    they come to be both humans and the tribes of other beasts
    at one time coming together into a single cosmos by Love   5
    and at another each being borne apart by the hatred of
        Strife,
    until they grow together into one, the whole, and become
        subordinate.
                    (Simplicius, *Commentary on Aristotle's Physics*
                                33.19–34.3 = 31B26)

51. But equal to itself on all sides, and wholly without limit,
    a rounded sphere, exulting in its circular solitude.
                        (Stobaeus, *Selections* 1.15.2 = 31B28)

52. By her [Love] many neckless faces sprouted,
    and arms were wandering naked, bereft of shoulders,
    and eyes were roaming alone, in need of foreheads.
                        (Simplicius, *Commentary on Aristotle's*
                            On the Heavens 586.12; 587.1–2 = 31B57)

53. [In this situation, the members were still] single-limbed
[as the result of the separation caused by Strife, and] they
wandered about [aiming at mixture with one another.]
(Simplicius, *Commentary on Aristotle's
On the Heavens* 587.18–19 = 31B58)

54. But when divinity was mixed to a greater extent with divinity,
and these things began to fall together, however they chanced
to meet,
and many others besides them arose continuously.
(Simplicius, *Commentary on Aristotle's
On the Heavens* 587.20; 23 = 31B59)

55. Many came into being with faces and chests on both sides,
man-faced ox-progeny, and some to the contrary rose up
as ox-headed things with the form of men, compounded
partly from men
and partly from women, fitted with shadowy parts.
(Aelian, *The Nature of Animals* 16.29 = 31B61)

56. For by earth we see earth, by water, water,
by aither, divine aither, and by fire, destructive fire,
yearning by yearning [Love] and strife by mournful Strife.
(Aristotle, *On the Soul* 404b11–15 = 31B109)

57. As when someone planning for a journey in the
wintry night
prepares a light, a gleam of blazing fire,
attaching a linen lantern against all the winds,
which scatters the blast of blowing winds,
but the light springs out, as much as it is finer,   5
and shines at the threshold with unwearying beams.
Thus at that time the original fire lay hidden
in the round pupil, enclosed in membranes and fine
garments
which are pierced straight through with marvelous
passages
which keep back the depth of water flowing around   10
but let the fire pass through as much as it is finer.
(Aristotle, *On the Senses* 437b24–438a5 = 31B84)

58. < The heart >, nurtured in the seas of rebounding blood,
    where most especially is what is called thought by humans,
    for the blood round the heart in humans is thought.
    (Porphyry, in Stobaeus, Selections I.49.53 = 31B105)

59. Narrow are the means of apprehension spread throughout
       the limbs.
    Many unhappy things burst in which blunt the thoughts.
    People see a tiny part of life during their time
    and swift-fated they are taken away and fly like smoke,
    persuaded only of whatever each of them has chanced to
       meet   5
    as they were driven everywhere; but everyone boasts that
       he discovered the whole.
    But these things are not in this way to be seen or heard by
       men
    or grasped with the mind. But you, since you have turned
       aside to this place,
    will learn; mortal cunning has reached no further.
    (Sextus Empiricus, Against the Mathematicians 7.123 = 31B2)

60. Blessed is he who possesses wealth of divine intelligence
    but wretched whose concern is a dim opinion about the gods.
    (Clement, Miscellanies 5.140 = 31B132)

61. There is an oracle of Necessity, an ancient decree of
       the gods,
    eternal and sealed with broad oaths,
    that whenever anyone pollutes his own dear limbs with
       the sin of murder,*
    . . . commits offense and swears a false oath—
    divinities (daimones) who possess immensely long life—   5
    he wanders away from the blessed ones for thrice ten
       thousand seasons,
    growing to be through time all different kinds of mortals
    taking the difficult paths of life one after another.
    For the force of aither pursues them to the sea
    and the sea spits them out onto the surface of the earth,
    and the earth into the rays   10

*Reading *phonoi* with most editors.

of the shining sun, and he [the sun] casts them into the
   vortices of aither.
One receives them after another, but all hate them.
Of them I am now one, a fugitive from the gods and
   a wanderer,
putting my reliance on raving Strife.
   (Hippolytus, *Refutation of All Heresies* 7.29.14–23 (lines 1–2,
   4–14); Plutarch, *On Exile* 607C (lines 1, 3, 5–16, 13) = 31B115)

62. But what is lawful for all extends far
through the wide-ruling aither and through the
   immense glare.
                    (Aristotle, *Rhetoric* I 1373b16–17 = 31B135)

63. Will you not cease from harsh-sounding murder?
   Do you not see
that you are devouring each other in the carelessness of
   your thought?
(Sextus Empiricus, *Against the Mathematicians* 9.129 = 31B136)

64. A father lifts up his own dear son who has
   changed form,
and, praying, slaughters him, committing a great folly.
   And they are at a loss,
sacrificing him as he entreats them. But he, refusing
   to hear the cries,
slaughters him and attends an evil feast in his halls.
Likewise a son seizes his father and children their mother
and tearing out their life devour the dear flesh.
(Sextus Empiricus, *Against the Mathematicians* 9.129 = 31B137)

65. Fast from evil.
                    (Plutarch, *The Control of Anger* 464B = 31B144)

ZENO OF ELEA

In his dialogue Parmenides *Plato tells us almost everything we know about Zeno. Zeno was about twenty-five years younger than Parmenides and was reputed to have been his lover. If Plato's chronology is accepted, Zeno was born about 490, and he and Parmenides visited Athens about 450, when Socrates was a young man of about twenty. The only other biographical story told about Zeno is that he resisted a tyranny and despite being tortured did not betray his comrades. Zeno explores the consequences of Parmenides' claims about what is. His ingenious arguments purport to show that neither plurality nor motion is compatible with Parmenides' requirements for being, and they have worried and fascinated philosophers from ancient times to the present. First, Zeno showed that the very postulation of a plurality of basic entities leads to difficulties, for if there were many things or if each thing that is had many characteristics, contradictions would follow: Things would be both like and unlike, both infinitely small and indefinitely large. Secondly, Zeno argued against the very possibility of motion or change, showing that the assumption of such motion results in contradictions.*

1. Once Parmenides and Zeno came to Athens for the Great
Panathenaic festival. Parmenides was quite an elderly man,
very grey, but fine and noble in appearance, just about sixty-
five years old. Zeno was then almost forty, of a good height and
handsome to see. The story goes that he had been Parmenides'
young lover. . . . Socrates and many others [were] eager to
listen to Zeno's treatise, for he had then brought it to Athens
for the first time. Socrates was then very young. Zeno himself
read it to them. . . . When Socrates had heard it, he asked
Zeno to read again the first hypothesis of the first argument.
When he had read it, he said, "How do you mean this, Zeno? If
things that are are many, they must therefore be both like and

127
b

c

d
e

unlike, but this is impossible. For unlike things cannot be like, nor can like things be unlike. Isn't that what you are saying?"

ZENO: Yes.

SOCRATES: Now if it is impossible for unlike things to be like and like things unlike, is it also possible for things to be many? For if they were many they would have impossible attributes. Is this the point of your arguments — to contend, against all that is said, that things are not many? And do you think that each of your arguments proves this . . . ?

128   ZENO: You have well understood the purpose of the whole work.

SOCRATES: I understand, Parmenides, that Zeno here wants to be identified with you by his treatise as well as his friendship, for he has written in the same style as you, but by

b   changing it he is trying to make us think he is saying something else. For in your poem you declare that the all is one and you do a good job of proving this, while he declares that it is not many, and furnishes many impressive proofs. Now when one of you says it is one and the other that it is not many, and each speaks so as to seem not to have said any of the same things, though you are saying practically the same things, what you have said appears beyond the rest of us.

ZENO: Yes, Socrates, but you have not completely understood the truth of the treatise. . . .

c   It is actually a defense of Parmenides' argument against those

d   who make fun of it, saying that if it is one, the argument has many ridiculous consequences which contradict it. Now my treatise opposes the advocates of plurality, and pays them back the same and more, aiming to prove that their hypothesis, "if there is a many," suffers still more ridiculous consequences than the hypothesis that there is one, if anyone follows it through sufficiently. I wrote it in this spirit of competitiveness when I was young, and then someone stole it, so I did not even have the chance to consider whether it should be made public.

     (Plato, *Parmenides* 127b–128d; part = 29A11, part = 29A2)

2. Zeno stated that if anyone could make clear to him what the one is, he would be able to speak of existing things.

     (Eudemus, *Physics* fr. 7, quoted in Simplicius,
     Commentary on Aristotle's Physics 97.12–13 = 29A16)

3. For if it should be added to something else that exists, it would not make it any bigger. For if it were of no size and was added, it [the thing it is added to] cannot increase in size. And so it follows immediately that what is added is nothing. But if when it is subtracted, the other thing is no smaller, nor is it increased when it is added, clearly the thing being added or subtracted is nothing.   (Simplicius, *Commentary on Aristotle's Physics* 139.11–15 = 29B2)

4. But if it exists, each thing must have some size and thickness, and part of it must be apart from the rest. And the same reasoning holds concerning the part that is in front. For that too will have size and part of it will be in front. Now it is the same thing to say this once and to keep saying it forever. For no such part of it will be last, nor will there be one part < of any such part > not related to another. Therefore, if there are many things, they must be both small and large; so small as not to have size, but so large as to be unlimited.
(Simplicius, *Commentary on Aristotle's Physics* 141.2–8 = 29B1)

5. If there are many, they must be just as many as they are and neither more nor less than that. But if they are as many as they are, they would be limited. If there are many, things that are are unlimited. For there are always others between the things that are, and again others between those, and so the things that are are unlimited.   (Simplicius, *Commentary on Aristotle's Physics* 140.29–33 = 29B3)

6. Zeno's arguments about motion which present difficulties for those who try to solve them are four. First is the argument which says that there is no motion because that which is moving must reach the midpoint before the end.
(Aristotle, *Physics* 6.9 239b9–13 = 29A25)

7. The second is the one called "Achilles." This is to the effect that the slowest as it runs will never be caught by the quickest. For the pursuer must first reach the point from which the pursued departed, so that the slower must always be some distance in front. This is the same argument as The Dichotomy, but it differs in not dividing the given magnitude in half.
(Aristotle, *Physics* 6.9 239b14–20 = 29A26)

8. For this reason Zeno's argument falsely assumes that it is impossible to traverse or come into contact with an infinite number of things individually in a finite time. For both length and time and generally everything that is continuous are called infinite in two ways: infinite in division and infinite with respect to their extremities. Now it is impossible to come into contact with things infinite in quantity in a finite time, but it is possible to do so with things that are infinite in division. For time itself too is infinite in this way. And so, it follows that it traverses the infinite in an infinite and not a finite time, and comes into contact with infinite things in infinite, not finite times.   (Aristotle, *Physics* 6.2 233a21–31 = 29A25)

9. This solution is sufficient to use against the person who raised the question (for he asked whether it is possible to traverse or count infinite things in a finite time), but insufficient for the facts of the matter and the truth.
                          (Aristotle, *Physics* 8.8 263a15–18, not in DK)

10. The third argument is the one just stated, that the arrow is stopped while it is moving. This follows from assuming that time is composed of "nows." If this is not conceded, the deduction will not go through.
                          (Aristotle, *Physics* 6.9 239b30–33 = 29A27)

Zeno makes a mistake in reasoning. For if, he says, everything is always at rest when it occupies a space equal to itself, and what is moving is always "in the now," the moving arrow is motionless.   (Aristotle, *Physics* 6.9 239b5–7 = 29A27)

11. The fourth argument is about the equal bodies moving in a stadium past equal bodies in the opposite direction, the one group moving from the end of the stadium, the other from the middle, at equal speed. He claims in this argument that it follows that half the time is equal to the double. The mistake is in thinking that an equal magnitude moving with equal speed takes an equal time in passing something moving as it does in passing something at rest. But this is false. Let *A*'s represent the equal stationary bodies, *B*'s represent the bodies beginning from the middle of the *A*'s, equal in number and size to

the A's, and C's represent the bodies beginning from the end, equal in number and size to these and having the same speed as the B's. It follows that the first B is at the end at the same time as the first C, as they [the B's and C's] move past each other, and the < first > C has passed by all the B's but the B's have passed half the A's. And so the time is half. For each of them is next to each thing for an equal time. It follows simultaneously that the B's have passed by all the C's, for the first C and the first B will be at the ends at the same time, because both have been next to the A's for an equal time.

(Aristotle, *Physics* 6.9 239b33–240a17 = 29A28)

12. If place exists, where is it? For everything that exists is in a place. Therefore, place is in a place. This goes on to infinity. Therefore, place does not exist.

(Simplicius, *Commentary on Aristotle's Physics* 562.3–6
(= 29B5); Aristotle, *Physics* 4.3 210b22–23, 4.1 209a23–25;
Eudemus, *Physics* fr. 42, quoted by Simplicius,
Commentary on Aristotle's Physics 563.25–28
(all three testimonia = 29A24))

13. ZENO: "Tell me, Protagoras, does a single millet seed make a noise when it falls, or one ten-thousandth of a millet seed?"
PROTAGORAS: "No."
ZENO: "Does a bushel of millet seeds make a noise when it falls, or doesn't it?"
PROTAGORAS: "It does."
ZENO: "But isn't there a ratio between the bushel of millet seeds and one millet seed, or one ten-thousandth of a millet seed?"
PROTAGORAS: "Yes there is."
ZENO: "So won't there be the same ratios of their sounds to one another? For as the things that make the noise < are to one another >, so are the noises < to one another >. But since this is so, if the bushel of millet seeds makes a noise, so will a single millet seed and one ten-thousandth of a millet seed."

(Simplicius, *Commentary on Aristotle's Physics*
1108.18–25 = 29A29)

ATOMISM: LEUCIPPUS AND DEMOCRITUS

Almost nothing is known of Leucippus, who was the first atomist. His birthplace was variously given as Miletus, Abdera, and Elea, and he was said to have written two books: On Mind *and* The Great World System. *Epicurus, a post-Aristotelian philosopher who adopted certain elements of Presocratic atomism, even denied that Leucippus existed at all. The tradition is that Leucippus was the teacher of Democritus, and this is one time when the tradition is undoubtedly correct. Democritus himself tells us that he was young when Anaxagoras was an old man (68B5), and so Democritus' birthdate is usually placed at around 460. He was born in Abdera in Thrace in Northern Greece (a birthplace he shared with Protagoras), but traveled throughout the ancient world (later sources even say he went to India, but this is doubtful). There are at least seventy titles of books written by Democritus on all sorts of subjects to be found in the ancient sources, both philosophical (on ethics, mathematics, natural philosophy, literature, and grammar) and more popular (for instance, he apparently wrote books based on his travels). There are also reports of books on medicine, farming, military science, and even painting. One of his books was called* The Little World System, *in obvious homage to his teacher Leucippus. The selections included here concentrate on the metaphysical and scientific theory known as atomism, expounded by both Leucippus and Democritus. Most of the evidence we have for the tenets of atomism come from Aristotle and the commentators on Aristotle; we have to keep in mind that some of these reports also involve interpretation. The word "atomos" in Greek means "uncuttable," and so atoms are things that cannot be cut up or actually divided or split. The atomists claimed that there were an infinite number of these atoms, each of which was uniform, eternal, and unchangeable (and so a genuine being in the Parmenidean sense). Individual atoms are imperceptible and differ from one another only in shape and size. These atoms move in a void—the word for "void" in Greek means "empty." The atomists identified the void with the "nothing" or "not-being" that Parmenides had proscribed. But it should be noted that*

the atomists insisted that nothing or not-being (the void) was real,
rather than just the negation of what is. Void allowed the atoms to move
and to come together without melding into one another. In reality, atoms
never touch, but simply come very close to one another as they move in
the void. The coming together and separating of atoms (the real, and ba-
sic, entities of the theory) is responsible for all the aspects of the sensible
world, and so what looks like coming to be or passing away is really only
alteration and rearrangement. As Democritus says, "By convention
sweet, by convention bitter; by convention hot, by convention cold; by
convention color; but in reality: atoms and the void" (B9). And, he
might have added, by convention air, by convention water, but in reality
atoms and the void. Democritus apparently thought that his atomic the-
ory could cover all aspects of life as we know it, and there are many
fragments on ethical matters attributed to him.

1. No thing happens at random but all things as a result of a
   reason and by necessity.   (Aetius 1.25.4 = 67B2)

2. Democritus leaves aside purpose, but refers all things which
   nature employs to necessity.
            (Aristotle, *Generation of Animals* 5.8 789b2–4 = 68A66)

   < Concerning necessity > Democritus < speaks of > knocking
   against < each other > and motion and "blow" of matter.
                                            (Aetius 1.26.2 = 68A66)

3. Leucippus and his associate Democritus declare the full and
   the empty [void] to be the elements, calling the former "what
   is" and the other "what is not." Of these the one, "what is," is
   full and solid, the other, "what is not," is empty [void] and
   rare. (This is why they say that what is is no more than what is
   not, because the void is no less than body is.) These are the
   material causes of existing things. . . . They declare that the
   differences < among these > are the causes of the rest. Moreover, they say that the differences are three: shape, arrangement, and position. For they say that what is differs only in
   "rhythm," "touching," and "turning" – and of these "rhythm"
   is shape, "touching" is arrangement, and "turning" is position.

For *A* differs from *N* in shape, *AN* from *NA* in arrangement, and *Z* from *N* in position. Concerning the origin and manner of motion in existing things, these men too, like the rest, lazily neglected to give an account.

(Aristotle, *Metaphysics* 1.4 985b4–20 = 67A6)

4. After making the shapes, Democritus and Leucippus make alteration and coming to be out of them: coming to be and destruction by means of separation and combination, alteration by means of arrangement and position. Since they held that the truth is in the appearance, and appearances are opposite and unlimited, they made the shapes unlimited, so that by reason of changes of the composite, the same thing seems opposite to different people, and it shifts position when a small amount is mixed in, and it appears completely different when one thing shifts position. For tragedy and comedy come to be out of the same letters. (Aristotle, *On Generation and Corruption* 1.2 315b6–15 = 67A97)

5. Democritus believes that the nature of the eternal things is small beings unlimited in multitude. As a place for these he hypothesizes something else, unlimited in size, and he calls the place by the names "void," "nothing" and "unlimited" [or, "infinite"] and he calls each of the substances "hing" and "compact" and "what is." He holds that the substances are so small that they escape our senses. They have all kinds of forms and shapes and differences in size. Out of these as elements he generates and combines visible and perceptible bodies. < These substances > contend with one another and move in the void on account of their dissimilarity and the other differences I have mentioned, and as they move they strike against one another and become entangled in a way that makes them be in contact and close to one another, but does not make any thing out of them that is truly one, for it is quite foolish < to think > that two or more things could ever come to be one. The grounds he gives for why the substances stay together up to a point are that the bodies fit together and hold each other fast. For some of them are rough, some are hooked, others concave and others convex, while yet others have innumerable other differences. So he thinks that they cling to each other and stay

together until some stronger necessity comes along from the environment and shakes them and scatters them apart. He describes the generation and its contrary, separation, not only for animals but also for plants, *cosmoi,* and altogether for all perceptible bodies.

(Aristotle, *On Democritus,* quoted by Simplicius, *Commentary on Aristotle's On the Heavens* 295.1–22 = 68A37)

6. Leucippus . . . did not follow the same path as Parmenides and Xenophanes concerning things that are, but seemingly the opposite one. For while they made the universe one, immovable, ungenerated, and limited, and did not even permit the investigation of what is not, he posited the atoms as unlimited and ever moving elements, and an unlimited multitude of shapes among them on the grounds that they are no more like this than like that, since he observed that coming to be and change are unceasing in things that are. Further, he posited that what is is no more than what is not, and both are equally causes of what comes to be. For supposing the substance of the atoms to be compact and full, he said it is "being" and that it moves in the void, which he called "not-being" and which he declares is no less than what is. His associate, Democritus of Abdera, likewise posited the full and the void as principles, of which he calls the former "being" and the latter "not-being." For positing the atoms as matter for the things that are they generate the rest by means of their differences. These are three: rhythm, turning, and touching, i.e., shape, position, and arrangement. For like is by nature moved by like, and things of the same kind move towards one another, and each of the shapes produces a different composition when arranged in a different compound. Thus, since the principles are unlimited, they reasonably promised to account for all attributes and substances—how and through what cause anything comes to be. This is why they say that only those who make the elements unlimited account for everything reasonably. They say that the multitude of the shapes among the atoms is unlimited on the grounds that they are no more like this than like that. For they themselves assign this as a cause of the unlimitedness.

(Simplicius, *Commentary on Aristotle's Physics* 28.4–26 = 67A8 = 68A38)

7. They declare that their nature is one, as if each were a separate
   piece of gold.   (Aristotle, *On the Heavens*
                                      1.7 275b32–276a1 = 67A19)

8. Plato and Democritus supposed that only the intelligible
   things are true; Democritus < held this view > because there
   is by nature no perceptible substrate, whereas the atoms,
   which combine to form all things, have a nature deprived of
   every perceptible quality.   (Sextus Empiricus, *Against the
                                      Mathematicians* 8.6 = 68A59)

9. Democritus specified two < basic properties of atoms >: size
   and shape; and Epicurus added weight as a third.
                                      (Aetius 1.3.18 = 68A47)

10. These men [Leucippus, Democritus, and Epicurus] said that
    the principles are unlimited in multitude, and they believed
    them to be atoms and indivisible and incapable of being acted
    upon because they are compact and have no share of void.
    (For they claimed that division occurs where there is void in
    bodies.) These atoms, which are separate from one another in
    the unlimited void and differ in shape and size and position,
    and arrangement, move in the void, and when they overtake
    one another they collide, and some rebound in whatever
    direction they may happen to, but others become entangled in
    virtue of the relation of their shapes, sizes, positions, and
    arrangements, and stay together, and this is how compounds
    are produced.   (Simplicius, *Commentary on Aristotle's
                           On the Heavens* 242.18–26 = 67A14)

11. Those who abandoned division to infinity on the grounds that
    we cannot divide to infinity and as a result cannot guarantee
    that the division cannot end, declared that bodies are com-
    posed of indivisible things and are divided into indivisibles.
    Except that Leucippus and Democritus hold that the cause of
    the primary bodies' indivisibility is not only their inability to
    be affected but also their minute size and lack of parts.
                           (Simplicius, *Commentary on Aristotle's Physics*
                           925.10–15 = 67A13)

12. Democritus would appear to have been persuaded by arguments that are relevant and appropriate to the science of nature. The point will be clear as we proceed. For there is a difficulty in supposing that there is some body, a magnitude, that is everywhere divisible and that this [the complete division] is possible. For what will there be that escapes the division? . . . Now since such a body is everywhere divisible, let it be divided. What, then, will be left? A magnitude? But this cannot be. For there will be something that has not been divided, whereas we supposed that it was everywhere divisible. But if there will be no body or magnitude left and yet the division will take place, either < the original body > will consist of points and its components will be without magnitude, or it will be nothing at all, so that it could come to be out of nothing and be composed of nothing, and the whole thing would then be nothing but an appearance. Likewise, if it is composed of points, it will not be a quantity. For when they were in contact and there was a single magnitude and they coincided, they made the whole thing none the larger. For when it is divided into two or more, the whole is no smaller or larger than before. And so, even if all the points are put together they will not make any magnitude. . . . These problems result from supposing that any body whatever of any size is everywhere divisible. . . . And so, since magnitudes cannot be composed of contacts or points, it is necessary for there to be indivisible bodies and magnitudes.   (Aristotle, *On Generation and Corruption* 1.2 316a13–b16 = 68A48b)

13. When Democritus said that the atoms are in contact with each other, he did not mean contact strictly speaking . . . but the condition in which the atoms are near one another and not far apart is what he called contact. For no matter what, they are separated by the void.
          (Philoponus, *Commentary on Aristotle's On Generation and Corruption* 158.27–159.3 = 67A7)

14. . . . when [Democritus] declares that the thing is no more than the nothing, he is calling body thing and void nothing, and declaring that this too [void] has some nature and existence of its own.   (Plutarch, *Against Colotes* 4.1109A = 68B156, tr. Curd)

15. People mean by void an interval in which there is no perceptible body. Since they believe that everything that is is body,
they say that void is that in which there is nothing at all. . . .
So it is necessary to prove . . . that there is no interval different from bodies . . . which breaks up the whole body so that
it is not continuous, as Democritus and Leucippus say, and
many other natural philosophers, or anything outside the
whole body, which is continuous. They say that there would
be no change in place (i.e., motion and growth), since motion
would not seem to exist if there were no void, since what is
full cannot admit anything. . . . Some things are seen to con-
tract and be compressed; for example, they say that the jars
hold the wine along with the wineskins, since the compressed
body contracts into the voids that are in it. Further all believe
that growth takes place through void, since the nourishment
is a body and two bodies cannot be together. They also use as
evidence what happens with ash, which receives as much
water as the empty vessel.
$\qquad$ (Aristotle, *Physics* 4.6 213a27–b22 = 67A19)

16. For they say that there is always motion. But they do not say
why or what motion it is, nor, if it is of one sort or another, do
they state the cause. $\qquad$ (Aristotle, *Metaphysics*
$\qquad$ 12.6 1071b33–35 = 67A18)

17. Leucippus and Democritus said that their primary bodies,
the atoms, are always moving in the unlimited void by com-
pulsion. $\qquad$ (Simplicius, *Commentary on Aristotle's On the
Heavens* 583.18–20 = 67A16)

18. Democritus, saying that the atoms are naturally motionless,
declares that they move "by a blow."
$\qquad$ (Simplicius, *Commentary on Aristotle's Physics*
$\qquad$ 42.10–11 = 68A47)

Democritus says that the primary bodies (these are the compact things) do not possess weight but move by knocking
against one another in the unlimited, and there can be an
atom the size of the cosmos. $\qquad$ (Aetius 1.12.6 = 68A47)

Democritus indicated a single type of motion, that due to vibration.   (Aetius 1.23.3 = 68A47)

19. What does Democritus say? That substances unlimited in multitude, atomic and not different in kind, and moreover incapable of acting or being acted upon, are in motion, scattered in the void. When they approach one another or collide or become entangled, the compounds appear as water or fire or as a plant or a human, but all things are atoms, which he calls forms; there is nothing else. For from what is not there is no coming to be, and nothing could come to be from things that are because on account of their hardness the atoms are not acted upon and do not change.   (Plutarch, *Against Colotes* 8 1110F–1111A = 68A57)

20. He makes sweet that which is round and good-sized; astringent that which is large, rough, polygonal, and not rounded; sharp tasting, as its name indicates, that which is sharp in body, and angular, bent and not rounded; pungent that which is round and small and angular and bent; salty that which is angular and good-sized and crooked and equal sided; bitter that which is round and smooth, crooked and small sized; oily that which is fine and round and small.
(Theophrastus, *Causes of Plants* 6.1.6 = 68A129)

21. None the less he is found condemning them [the senses]. For he says, "We in fact understand nothing exactly [or, exact], but what changes according to the disposition both of the body and of the things that enter it and offer resistance to it."
(Sextus Empiricus, *Against the Mathematicians* 7.136 = 68B9)

22. There are two kinds of judgment, one legitimate and the other bastard. All the following belong to the bastard: sight, hearing, smell, taste, touch. The other is legitimate and is separated from this. When the bastard one is unable to see or hear or smell or taste or grasp by touch any further in the direction of smallness, but < we need to go still further > towards what is fine, < then the legitimate one enables us to carry on >.
(Sextus Empiricus, *Against the Mathematicians* 7.138 = 68B11)

23. A person must know by this rule that he is separated from reality. (Sextus Empiricus, *Against the Mathematicians* 7.136 = 68B6)

24. In fact it will be clear that to know in reality what each thing is like is a matter of perplexity. (Sextus Empiricus, *Against the Mathematicians* 7.136 = 68B8)

25. In reality we know nothing about anything, but for each person opinion is a reshaping [of the soul atoms by the atoms entering from without]. (Sextus Empiricus, *Against the Mathematicians* 7.136 = 68B7)

26. By convention [or, custom], sweet; by convention, bitter; by convention, hot; by convention, cold; by convention, color; but in reality, atoms and void.
(Sextus Empiricus, *Against the Mathematicians* 7.135 = 68B9 (= B125))

27. Wretched mind, after taking your evidence from us do you throw us down? Throwing us down is a fall for you!
(Galen, *On Medical Experience* 15.8 = 68B125; B125 also includes a restatement of B9)

28. Cheerfulness arises in people through moderation of enjoyment and due proportion in life. Deficiencies and excesses tend to change suddenly and give rise to large movements in the soul. Souls which undergo motions involving large intervals are neither steady nor cheerful. . . .
(Stobaeus, *Selections* 3.1.210 = 68B191)

29. Accept nothing pleasant unless it is beneficial.
(Democrates, *Maxims* = 68B74)

30. To all humans the same thing is good and true, but different people find different things pleasant.
(Democrates, *Maxims* = 68B69)

31. Best for a person is to live his life being as cheerful and as little
    distressed as possible. This will occur if he does not make his
    pleasures in mortal things.

    (Stobaeus, *Selections* 3.1.47 = 68B189)

32. All those who make their pleasures from the belly, exceeding
    the right time for food, drink, or sex, have short-lived plea-
    sures — only for as long as they eat or drink — but many pains.

    (Stobaeus, *Selections* 3.18.35 = 68B235)

MELISSUS

Melissus of Samos was an admiral as well as a philosopher. Although he lived on Samos (the island in the eastern Aegean that was the original home of Pythagoras), he adopted the philosophy of Elea, accepting the arguments of Parmenides. We do not know his birthdate, but in 441 he defeated the Athenian navy under Pericles. Melissus' treatise is a sustained exploration of the consequences of Parmenides' thought. He argues that there can be only one thing, and that among other characteristics, this One—as he called it—must be changeless (thus ruling out Milesian material monism), full (thus rejecting the void), not subject to density and rarity (thus banning a system like Anaximenes', in which a single basic stuff undergoes changes in density to become everything else), and not subject to rearrangement (a possible attack on atomism). Further, it can have no body, although Melissus also, rather oddly, says that the One is indefinite in magnitude. Melissus was roundly abused by Aristotle, but he sets out his arguments clearly and exploits the consequences of Parmenides' argument that only what is can be.

1. Whatever was, always was and always will be. For if it came to be, it is necessary that before it came to be it was nothing. Now if it was nothing, in no way could anything come to be out of nothing. (Simplicius, *Commentary on Aristotle's Physics* 162.23–26 = 30B1)

2. Now since it did not come to be, it is and always was and always will be, and does not have a beginning or an end, but is unlimited. For if it had come to be it would have a beginning (for having come to be it would have begun at some time) and an end (for having come to be it would have ended at some time). But since it neither began nor ended, it always was and

89

always will be and does not have a beginning or end. For whatever is not entire cannot always be.

(Simplicius, *Commentary on Aristotle's Physics* 29.22–26, 109.20–25 = 30B2)

3. [Just as he says that what came to be at some time is limited in its being, he also wrote clearly that what always is is unlimited in being, saying:] But just as it always is, so also it must always be unlimited in magnitude. [But by "magnitude" he does not mean what is extended in space.]

(Simplicius, *Commentary on Aristotle's Physics* 109.29–32 = 30B3)

4. Nothing that has both a beginning and an end is either eternal or unlimited. And so whatever does not have them is unlimited.

(Simplicius, *Commentary on Aristotle's Physics* 110.2–4 = 30B4)

5. If it is not one, it will come to a limit against something else.

(Simplicius, *Commentary on Aristotle's Physics* 110.5–6 = 30B5)

6. For if it is < unlimited >, it will be one. For if there were two, they could not be unlimited, but would have limits against each other.   (Simplicius, *Commentary on Aristotle's On the Heavens* 557.14–17 = 30B6)

7. Thus it is eternal and unlimited and one and all alike.
And it cannot perish, or become greater, or be rearranged, or feel pain or distress. For if it experienced any of these, it would no longer be one. For if it became different, it is necessary that what is is not alike, but what previously was perishes, and what is not comes to be. Now if it should become different by one hair in ten thousand years, it will all perish in all of time.
But it is not possible for it to be rearranged, either. For the arrangement that previously was is not destroyed and an arrangement that is not does not come to be. But when nothing either comes to be in addition or is destroyed or becomes different, how could anything that is be rearranged? For if it became at all different, it would indeed already have been rearranged.

Nor does it feel pain. For it could not be all if it were feeling pain. For a thing feeling pain could not always be. Nor does it have equal power to what is healthy. Nor would it be alike if it were feeling pain. For it would feel pain because something is being taken away or added, and it would no longer be alike. Nor would what is healthy be able to feel pain. For what is healthy and what is would perish, and what is not would come to be.

And the same argument applies to feeling distress as to feeling pain.

Nor is any of it empty. For what is empty is nothing, and of course what is nothing would not be. Nor does it move. For it is not able to give way anywhere, but is full. For if it were empty it would give way into the empty. But since it is not empty, it does not have anywhere to give way.

It cannot be dense and rare. For it is impossible for the rare to be equally full as the dense, but the rare immediately proves to be emptier than the dense.

And it is necessary to make this the grounds for deciding whether something is full or not full: if something moves or can move, it is not full. But if it neither moves nor can move, it is full.

Now it is necessary that it is full if it is not empty. Now if it is full, it does not move.

(Simplicius, *Commentary on Aristotle's Physics*
111.18–112.15 = 30B7)

8. Now this argument is the strongest indication that it is only one.

But also the following are indications.

For if there were many, they would have to be such as I say the one is. For if there is earth and water and air and fire and iron and gold, and one thing is alive and another is dead, and black and white, and all the other things that people say are true, if indeed these are, and we see and hear correctly, each must be such as we decided at first, and must not change or come to be different, but each thing must always be just as it is. But as the case stands, we say we see and hear and understand correctly. We think that what is hot becomes cold and what is cold, hot, and what is hard becomes soft, and what is soft, hard, and what is alive dies and comes to be from what is not alive, and all these things become different, and anything that was and what is now are not at all alike, but iron, which is hard, is worn away by contact with the finger, and also gold and stone and anything else that seems to be strong, and earth and stone come to be from water.

Now these things do not agree with one another. For we say that there are many things that are eternal and have forms and strength, but all of them seem to us to become different and change from what we see at each moment.

Now it is clear that we were not seeing correctly and that that plurality does not correctly seem to be. For they would not change if they were real, but would be as each of them seemed. For nothing is stronger than what is real.

But if it changes, what is is destroyed, and what is not has come to be. Thus, if there are many, they must be like the one.

(Simplicius, *Commentary on Aristotle's On the Heavens* 558.19–559.12 = 30B8)

9. [That he intends what is to be bodiless he indicated, saying:] Now if it is, it must be one. But being one, it must not have body. But if it had thickness, it would have parts and no longer would be one.   (Simplicius, *Commentary on Aristotle's Physics* 109.34–110.2 = 30B9)

10. For he himself proves that what is is indivisible. For if what is is divided, it moves. But if it moved, it would not be. [But by "magnitude" he means the greatness of its being.]

(Simplicius, *Commentary on Aristotle's Physics* 109.32–34 = 30B10; rev. Curd)

11. Being one it is all alike. For if it were unlike, being plural, it would no longer be one, but many.

(pseudo-Aristotle, *On Melissus, Xenophanes and Gorgias* 1 974a12–14 = 30A5)

DIOGENES OF APOLLONIA

Theophrastus says that Diogenes of Apollonia was perhaps the last of the physiologoi, *philosophers who concentrated on the natural world. Diogenes was probably from Apollonia on the Black Sea, a colony of Miletus (although there is an Apollonia in Crete as well); the best evidence suggests that he was active after 440. This means that he was a contemporary of Melissus and Leucippus, although the chronology is very difficult to work out. There are references to his views in the plays of Euripides and Aristophanes and in Plato's* Phaedo. *Nothing is known of his life, although his interest in the role of the brain in perception and in the operation of the veins suggests that he may have been a medical man.* * *Simplicius had seen a copy of Diogenes' book called* On Nature *and suggests that he may have written at least three other books as well. In his theories Diogenes combines the material monism of the Milesians with an understanding of the Eleatic requirements on a theory of nature. He provides arguments against metaphysical pluralism and for monism (B2), and he attributes both divine and intelligent qualities to air, his one basic being. Everything is a form of air, which is altered through the mechanisms of condensation and rarefaction; the degree of intelligence a thing has is determined by the warmth of its internal air.*

1. In my opinion, a person beginning any discourse must present a starting point (or, principle) that is indisputable, and an explanation (or, style) that is simple and serious.
    (Diogenes Laertius, *Lives of the Philosophers* 9.57 = 64B1)

2. In my opinion, to sum it all up, all things that are, are differentiated from the same thing and are the same thing.

*Diogenes' account of the veins can be found in Aristotle, *History of Animals* 3.2 511b30–512b11 (64B6).

And this is manifest. For if the things that are now in this cosmos—earth, water, air, fire, and all the rest that are seen to exist in this cosmos—if any one of these were different from another, being different in its own nature, and if it were not the case that being the same thing it changed and was differentiated in many ways, they could not mix with each other in any way, nor could help or harm come to one from another, nor could a plant grow from the earth, nor an animal or anything else come to be, unless they were so constituted as to be the same thing.

But all these things, being differentiated out of the same thing, come to be different things at different times and return into the same thing.   (Simplicius, *Commentary on Aristotle's Physics* 151.31–152.7 = 64B2)

3. For without intelligence it could not be distributed in such a way as to have the measures of all things—winter and summer, night and day, rains and winds and good weather. If anyone wants to think about the other things too, he would find that as they are arranged, they are as good as possible.
     (Simplicius, *Commentary on Aristotle's Physics* 152.12–16 = 64B3)

4. Moreover, in addition to the preceding indications, the following too are important. Humans and animals live by means of air through breathing. And this (air) is both soul and intelligence for them, as will be displayed manifestly in this book. And if this departs, they die and their intelligence fails.
     (Simplicius, *Commentary on Aristotle's Physics* 152.18–21 = 64B4)

5. And in my opinion, that which possesses intelligence is what people call air, and all humans are governed by it and it rules all things.
   For in my opinion this very thing is god, and it reaches everything and arranges all things and is in everything.
   And there is no single thing which does not share in this.
   But no single thing shares in it in the same way as anything else, but there are many forms both of air itself and of intelligence.
   For it is multiform—hotter and colder, drier and wetter, more stable and possessing a sharper movement, and unlimitedly many other alterations are in it, both of flavor and of color.

And the soul of all animals is the same thing, air hotter than the air outside in which we are located, but much colder than the air near the sun.

This heat is not identical in any two animals, since it is not identical even in any two humans, but it differs—not greatly, but so that they are similar.

Moreover, it is impossible for any of the things that are being differentiated to be exactly like one another without becoming the same thing.

Now since the differentiation is multiform, also the animals are multiform and many and are like one another in neither shape nor way of life nor intelligence, on account of the large number of their differentiations.

Nevertheless, all things live, see, and hear by means of the same thing, and all get the rest of their intelligence from the same thing.   (Simplicius, *Commentary on Aristotle's Physics*
152.22–153.17 = 64B5)

6. And this very thing is an eternal and immortal body, and by means of it some things come to be and others pass away.
(Simplicius, *Commentary on Aristotle's Physics*
153.19–20 = 64B7)

7. But this seems clear to me, that it is large and strong and eternal and immortal and knowing many things.
(Simplicius, *Commentary on Aristotle's Physics*
153.20–22 = 64B8)

8. Air is the element. There are unlimited worlds and unlimited void. The air by being condensed and rarefied is generative of the worlds. Nothing comes to be from or perishes into what is not. The earth is round and is supported in the center (of the cosmos) and has undergone its process of formation through the rotation resulting from the hot and the solidification caused by the cold.   (Diogenes Laertius, *Lives of the Philosophers*
9.57 = 64A1)

9. All things are in motion and there are infinite worlds. His account of cosmogony is the following: the whole is in motion and comes to be rare in one place, dense in another. Where the

dense part chanced to come together it formed the earth by revolving, and the other things in the same way. The lightest things occupied the highest location and produced the sun.

(pseudo-Plutarch, *Miscellanies*, 12 = 64A6)

10. Diogenes attributes the senses, as well as life and thought, to air. . . . The sense of smell is due to the air around the brain. . . . Hearing occurs when the air in the ears is set in motion by the air outside and is passed on towards the brain. Sight occurs when things are reflected in the pupil, and this, being mixed with the air inside, produces sensation. Evidence of this is the fact that if the veins (in the eyes) become inflamed, it is not mixed with the air inside and we do not see, although the reflection is there just the same. Taste occurs in the tongue because of its rare and soft nature. Concerning touch he declared nothing, neither its functioning nor its objects. . . . The interior air, which is a small part of god, is what perceives. Evidence of this is that often when we have our mind on other matters we neither see nor hear.

Pleasure and pain arise in the following manner: pleasure whenever a large amount of air is mixed with the blood and makes it light, being in accordance with its nature and penetrating the whole body, and pain whenever the air is contrary to its nature and is not mixed, and the blood coagulates and becomes weaker and denser. Similarly also boldness and health and the opposites. . . . Thought, as was said, is due to air that is pure and dry. For moisture hinders the mind. For this reason thought is diminished when we are asleep, drunk, or full. . . . This is why children are foolish. . . . They are also prone to anger and in general easily roused and changeable because air, which is great in quantity, is separated by small intervals. This is also the cause of forgetfulness: when the air does not go through the entire body, people cannot comprehend.   (Theophrastus, *On the Senses* 39–45 = 64A19)

THE SOPHISTS

The individual Sophists included here are representatives of an important movement in fifth-century Greece. The Presocratic philosophers were mainly interested in natural philosophy, although many of them, notably Heraclitus, Empedocles, and Democritus, also explored issues in moral and social philosophy. The Sophists were fundamentally moral and social thinkers. The upheavals of the Peloponnesian War (431–404), a nearly thirty-year conflict, in which Athens was finally defeated by Sparta, had called many traditional values into question, and the growth of democracies (especially at Athens) called for a new civic virtue: the ability to speak well and persuasively in the assemblies and law courts. The Sophists explored all these issues. Most of them were itinerant teachers, taking on as pupils only those who could pay the fee (though this seems to have been the only requirement to be admitted as a pupil of a Sophist). They offered instruction in rhetorical skills (on almost any subject) and explored and exploited the new attitudes to traditional virtues. The Sophists examined the issue of whether morality was a matter of nature or convention; they gave rhetorical displays to large (and well-paying) crowds; and, according to Plato, many of them more than once crossed philosophical swords with Socrates, who was disdainful of their claims to many sorts of knowledge. They occupied an ambivalent position in Greek life, and on the evidence of Plato's dialogues, they were thought to be both fascinating and dangerous. Protagoras, the most famous of the early Sophists, was born in Abdera in Thrace, probably in 490 (about twenty years before Socrates), and he died about 420. He was often in Athens and became a part of the circle around Pericles, but he was also well known in the western Greek cities in Sicily and Southern Italy. His contemporary, Gorgias of Leontini (in Sicily), was almost as well known as Protagoras himself. Gorgias, too, was born around 490, and there are reports that he was well over one hundred when he died. There are also reports that he was a student of Empedocles, and he certainly shows an interest in metaphysical questions: One of his works is called On Not-Being. *The Sophist we know*

*as Antiphon is probably Antiphon of Rhamnous. As a native of Attica,
he could put his own teachings into practice in the Assembly and in
other gatherings that were limited to Athenian citizens. He was born
about 480 and apparently had wide philosophical and scientific interests
like others of the Presocratic philosophers. But it is as a Sophist that he
is best known, having published a work called* Tetralogies *which pur-
ported to teach how to make whichever side of a lawsuit one happens to
be arguing for the strongest. Critias, too, was an Athenian, a cousin to
Plato's mother, and an associate of Socrates. He was probably born
around 453. Critias was one of the Thirty Tyrants, steadfast opponents
of the democratic movement in Athens, and he died in 403 in the civil
war in Athens between the democrats and the oligarchs. He was not
technically a Sophist, for he was not a paid teacher but a politician. But
to many Athenians, Critias seemed a perfect product of the Sophistic
movement, representing both the glamour and the peril embodied in the
teachings and activities of the Sophists.*

Protagoras

1. A human being is the measure of all things – of things that are,
   that they are, and of things that are not, that they are not.
   (Sextus Empiricus, *Against the Mathematicians* 7.60 = 80B1)

2. Concerning the gods I am unable to know either that they are
   or that they are not, or what their appearance is like. For many
   are the things that hinder knowledge: the obscurity of the
   matter and the shortness of human life.
   (Eusebius, *Preparation of the Gospel* 14.3.7 = 80B4)

3. There are two opposing arguments (*logoi*) concerning everything.   (Diogenes Laertius, *Lives of the Philosophers*
                                      9.51 = 80B6a; tr. Curd)

4. To make the weaker argument (*logos*) the stronger.
   (Aristotle, *Rhetoric* 1402a23 = 80B6b; tr. Curd)

5. Education is not implanted in the soul unless one reaches a
   greater depth.   (Plutarch, *On Practice* 178.25 = 80B11)

Gorgias

6. He concludes as follows that nothing is: if [something] is, either   *66*
what-is is or what-is-not [is], or both what-is and what-is-not
are. But it is the case neither that what-is is, as he will show, nor
that what-is-not is, as he will justify, nor that both what-is and
what-is-not are, as he will teach this too. Therefore, it is not the   *67*
case that anything is. And in fact, what-is-not is not. For if
what-is-not is, it will be and not be at the same time. For in that
it is considered as not being, it will not be, but in that it *is* not
being, on the other hand, it will be. But it is completely absurd
that something be and not be at the same time. Therefore, it is
not the case that what-is-not is. And differently: if what-is-not
is, what-is will not be, since they are opposites, and if being is
an attribute of what-is-not, not-being will be an attribute of
what-is. But it is certainly not the case that what-is is not, and
so neither will what-is-not be. Further, neither is it the case that   *68*
what-is is. For if what-is is, it is either eternal or generated or
eternal and generated at the same time. But it is neither eternal
nor generated nor both, as we will show. Therefore it is not the
case that what-is is. For if what-is is eternal (we must begin at
this point), it does not have any beginning. For everything that   *69*
comes to be has some beginning, but what is eternal, being
ungenerated, did not have a beginning. But if it does not have a
beginning, it is unlimited, and if it is unlimited it is nowhere.
For if it is anywhere, that in which it is is different from it, and
so what-is will no longer be unlimited, since it is enclosed in
something. For what encloses is larger than what is enclosed,
but nothing is larger than what is unlimited, and so what is   *70*
unlimited is not anywhere. Further, it is not enclosed in itself,
either. For "that in which" and "that in it" will be the same, and
what-is will become two, place and body (for "that in which" is
place, and "that in it" is body). But this is absurd, so what-is is
not in itself, either. And so, if what-is is eternal, it is unlimited,
but if it is unlimited it is nowhere, and if it is nowhere it is not.
So if what-is is eternal, it is not at all. Further, what-is cannot   *71*
be generated either. For if it has come to be it did so either from
a thing that is or from a thing that is not. But it has come to be
neither from what-is (for if it is a thing that is, it has not come to
be, but already is), nor from what-is-not (for what-is-not cannot

generate anything, since what generates anything must of
necessity share in existence). Therefore, it is not the case that
72   what-is is generated either. In the same ways, it is not both
eternal and generated at the same time. For these exclude one
another, and if what-is is eternal it has not come to be, and if it
has come to be it is not eternal. So if what-is is neither eternal
73   nor generated nor both together, what-is would not be. And
differently, if it is, it is either one or many. But it is neither one
nor many, as will be shown. Therefore it is not the case that
what-is is. For if it is one, it is either a quantity or continuous or
a magnitude or a body. But whichever of these it is, it is not one,
but being a quantity, it will be divided, and if it is continuous it
will be cut. Similarly if conceived as a magnitude it will not be
indivisible. And if it chances to be a body, it will be three-
dimensional, for it will have length, width and depth. But it is
absurd to say that what-is is none of these. Therefore, it is not
74   the case that what-is is one. Further, it is not many. For if it is
not one, it is not many either. For the many is a compound of
individual ones, and so since [the thesis that what-is is] one is
refuted, [the thesis that what-is is] many is refuted along with
it. But it is altogether clear from this that neither what-is nor
75   what-is-not is. It is easy to conclude that neither is it the case
that both of them are, what-is and what-is-not. For if what-is-
not is and what-is is, then what-is-not will be the same as what-
is as regards being. And for this reason neither of them is. For it
is agreed that what-is-not is not, and what-is has been shown
76   to be the same as this. So it too will not be. However, if what-is
is the same as what-is-not, it is not possible for both to be. For if
both [are], then they are not the same, and if [they are] the
same, then [it is] not [the case that] both [are]. It follows that
nothing is. For if neither what-is is nor what-is-not nor both,
and nothing aside from these is conceived of, nothing is.
77   Next in order is to teach that even if something is, it is unknow-
able and inconceivable by humans. For if things that are
thought of, says Gorgias, are not things-that-are, what-is is not
thought of. And reasonably so. For just as if things that are
thought of have the attribute of being white, being thought of
would be an attribute of white things, so if things that are
thought of have the attribute of not being things-that-are, not
to be thought of will necessarily be an attribute of things-that-

are. This is why the claim that if things that are thought of are   *78*
not things-that-are, what-is is not thought of is sound and
preserves the sequence of argument. But things that are thought
of (for we must assume this) are not things-that-are, as we will
show. Therefore it is not the case that what-is is thought of.
Further, it is completely clear that things that are thought of are
not things-that-are. For if things that are thought of are things-   *79*
that-are, all things that are thought of are—indeed, however
anyone thinks of them. But this is apparently false. For if
someone thinks of a person flying or chariots racing in the sea,
it is not the case that forthwith a person is flying or chariots
racing in the sea. And so, it is not the case that things that are
thought of are things-that-are. In addition, if things that are   *80*
thought of are things-that-are, things-that-are-not will not be
thought of. For opposites have opposite attributes, and what-
is-not is opposite to what-is. For this reason, if being thought of
is an attribute of what-is, not being thought of will assuredly be
an attribute of what-is-not. But this is absurd. For Scylla and
Chimaera and many things-that-are-not are thought of. Therefore it is not the case that what-is is thought of. And just as   *81*
things that are seen are called visible because they are seen and
things that are heard are called audible because they are heard,
and we do not reject visible things because they are not heard
or dismiss audible things because they are not seen (for each
ought to be judged by its own sense, not by another), so also
things that are thought of will be, even if they may not be seen
by vision or heard by hearing, because they are grasped by
their own criterion. So if someone thinks that chariots race in   *82*
the sea, even if he does not see them, he ought to believe that
there are chariots racing in the sea. But this is absurd. Therefore it is not the case that what-is is thought of and comprehended. But even if it should be comprehended, it cannot be   *83*
expressed to another. For if things-that-are are visible and
audible and generally perceptible, and in fact are external
objects, and of these the visible are comprehended by vision
and the audible by hearing, and not vice versa, how can these
be communicated to another? For that by which we communi-   *84*
cate is *logos*, but *logos* is not the objects, the things-that-are.
Therefore it is not the case that we communicate things-that-
are to our neighbors, but *logos*, which is different from the

objects. So just as the visible could not become audible and vice
versa, thus, since what-is is an external object, it could not
85   become our *logos*. But if it were not *logos*, it would not have been
revealed to another. In fact, *logos*, he says, is composed from
external things, i.e., perceptible things, falling upon us. For
from encountering flavor there arises in us the *logos* which is
expressed with reference to this quality, and from the inci-
dence on the senses of color arises the *logos* with reference to
color. But if so, it is not the *logos* that makes manifest the
external (object), but the external (object) that comes to be
86   communicative of the *logos*. Further, it is not possible to say
that *logos* is an object in the way visible and audible things are,
so that objects which are can be communicated by it, which is
an object which is. For, he says, even if *logos* is an object, it
anyway differs from all other objects, and visible bodies differ
most from *logos*. For the visible is grasped by one organ, *logos*
by another. Therefore it is not the case that *logos* makes manifest the great number of objects, just as they do not reveal the
nature of one another.
(Sextus Empiricus, *Against the Mathematicians* 7.65-86 = 82B3)

5   7. I will set forth the reasons for which it was likely that Helen's
6   voyage to Troy took place. She did what she did through the
will of Fate and the designs of the gods and decrees of Necessity or because she was taken by force, persuaded by words
8   (*logoi*), or conquered by Love. . . . Not even if speech (*logos*)
persuaded and deceived her soul, is it hard to make a defense
against this charge and free her from blame, as follows. *Logos* is
a powerful master, which by means of the smallest and most
invisible body accomplishes most divine deeds. For it can put
an end to fear, remove grief, instill joy, and increase pity. I will
9   prove how this is so. But it is to the opinion of my audience that
I must prove it. I both consider and define all poetry to be
speech (*logos*) with meter. Those who hear it are overcome with
fearful shuddering, tearful pity, and mournful yearning, and
over the good fortunes and ill-farings of other people and their
affairs the soul experiences a feeling of its own, through the
words (*logoi*). Come now, let me shift from one argument
10   (*logos*) to another. Inspired incantations bring on pleasure and
bring away grief through words (*logoi*). For conversing with the

soul's opinion the power of incantation charms, persuades, and changes it by witchcraft. Two arts of witchcraft and magic have been discovered – errors of the soul and deceptions of   11
opinion. All who have persuaded or who persuade anyone of anything do so by fashioning false *logos*. For if on all subjects everyone had memory of the past, [a conception] of the present and foreknowledge of the future, *logos* would not be similarly similar as it is for people who, as things are, cannot easily remember the past, consider the present or divine the future. Thus, on most matters, most people make opinion an adviser to their soul. But opinion is fallible and uncertain, and involves those who make use of it in fallible and uncertain successes.   12
What, then, keeps us from supposing that Helen too, against her will, came under the influence of *logoi* just as if she had been taken by the force of mighty men? For it was possible to see how persuasion prevails, which lacks the appearance of necessity but has the same power. For *logos*, which persuaded, compelled the soul, which it persuaded, both to believe what was said and to approve what was done. Therefore, the one who persuaded, since he compelled, is unjust, and the one who was persuaded, since she was compelled by *logos*, is wrongly blamed. As to the fact that persuasion added to *logos*   13
makes whatever impression it likes on the soul, one should attend first to the accounts (*logoi*) of the astronomers, who replace one opinion with another and so make things incredible and unclear seem apparent to the eyes of opinion; second, to compulsory competitions which use speeches (*logoi*), in which a single *logos* written with art but not spoken with truth delights and persuades a large crowd; and third, to contests of philosophers' accounts (*logoi*), in which is revealed how easily the swiftness of thought makes our confidence in our opinion change. The power of *logos* has the same relation (*logos*) to the   14
order of the soul as the order of drugs has to the nature of bodies. For as different drugs expel different humors from the body, and some put an end to sickness and others to life, so some *logoi* cause grief, others joy, some fear, others render their hearers bold, and still others drug and bewitch the soul through   15
an evil persuasion. It has been stated that if she was persuaded by *logos* she did not do wrong but was unfortunate. . . . By my   21
account (*logos*) I have removed ill fame from a woman. I have

stayed faithful to the rule I stipulated at the beginning of my
logos. I have attempted to put an end to the injustice of blame
and ignorance of opinion. I wanted to write the *logos* as a
praise of Helen and an entertainment for myself.

(Encomium of Helen = 82B11)

8. Gorgias said that one should destroy the seriousness of one's
opponent with laughter, and his laughter with seriousness.

(Aristotle, Rhetoric 1419b3 = 82B12;
tr. Curd, with Reeve and Cohen)

9. [Gorgias said that tragedy creates a deception in which] the
deceiver is more just than the nondeceiver and the deceived is
wiser than the undeceived.

(Plutarch, On the Fame of the Athenians 5.348c = 82B23;
tr. Curd, with Reeve and Cohen)

10. Those who do not care for philosophy, but engage in ordinary
studies are like the suitors, who wanted Penelope but slept
with her handmaids.

(Gnomologium Vaticanum 743 n.166 = 82B29;
tr. Curd, with Reeve and Cohen)

Antiphon

11. Understanding these things you will know that there is for
[the mind] not one of the things the person seeing farthest
sees with his vision, nor of the things the person knowing
most profoundly knows.

(Galen, Commentary on Hippocrates' The Doctor's
Workshop 18B656 = 87B1;
tr. Curd, with Reeve and Cohen)

12. In all human beings the mind leads the body into health or
disease or anything else.

(Galen, Commentary on Hippocrates' The Doctor's
Workshop 18B656 = 87B2;
tr. Curd, with Reeve and Cohen)

13. Time is a thought or a measure, not a reality.
>(Aetius, 1.22.6 = 87B9;
>tr. Curd, with Reeve and Cohen)

14. Because of this, god does not need anything nor does he receive anything from anyone, but he is boundless and lacks nothing.
>(Suda v. adeētos = 87B10;
>tr. Curd, with Reeve and Cohen)

15. If someone were to bury a bed and the rotting wood came to life, it would become not a bed, but a tree.
>(Harpocration, Lexicon v. embios = 87B15;
>tr. Curd, with Reeve and Cohen)

16. . . . Justice is a matter of not transgressing what the laws prescribe in whatever city you are a citizen of. A person would make most advantage of justice for himself if he treated the laws as important in the presence of witnesses, and treated the decrees of nature as important when alone and with no witnesses present. For the decrees of laws are extra additions, those of nature are necessary; those of the laws are the products of agreement, not of natural growth, whereas those of nature are the products of natural growth, not of agreement. If those who made the agreement do not notice a person transgressing the prescriptions of laws, he is free from both disgrace and penalty, but not so if they do notice him. But if, contrary to possibility, anyone violates any of the things which are innate by nature, the evil is no less if no one notices him and no greater if all observe. For he does not suffer harm as a result of opinion, but as a result of truth.

This is the entire purpose of considering these matters—that most of the things that are just according to law are established in a way which is hostile to nature. For laws have been established for the eyes, as to what they must see and what they must not, and for the ears, as to what they must hear and what they must not, and for the tongue, as to what it must say and what it must not, and for the hands, as to what they must do and what they must not, and for the feet, as to where they must go and where they must not, and for the mind, as to what it must desire and what it must not. Now the things from which the laws deter humans are no more in accord with or suited to nature than the things which they promote.

Living and dying are matters of nature, and living results for them from what is advantageous, dying from what is not advantageous. But the advantages which are established by the laws are bonds on nature, and those established by nature are free.

And so, things that cause distress, at least when thought of correctly, do not help nature more than things that give joy. Therefore, it will not be painful things rather than pleasant things which are advantageous. For things that are truly advantageous must not cause harm but benefit. Now the things that are advantageous by nature are among these. . . .

<But according to law, those are correct> who defend themselves after suffering and are not first to do wrong, and those who do good to parents who are bad to them, and who permit others to accuse them on oath but do not themselves accuse on oath. You will find most of these cases hostile to nature. They permit people to suffer more pain when less is possible and to have less pleasure when more is possible, and to receive injury when it is not necessary.

Now if some assistance came from the laws for those who submitted to these conditions and some damage to those who do not submit but resist, obedience to the laws would not be unhelpful. But as things are, it is obvious that the justice that stems from law is insufficient to rescue those who submit. In the first place, it permits the one who suffers to suffer and the wrongdoer to do wrong, and it was not at the time of the wrongdoing able to prevent either the sufferer from suffering or the wrongdoer from doing wrong. And when the case is brought to trial, there is no special advantage for the one who has suffered over the wrongdoer. For he must persuade the jury that he suffered and that he is able to exact the penalty. And it is open to the wrongdoer to deny it. . . . However convincing the accusation is on behalf of the accuser, the defense can be just as convincing. For victory comes through speech.

(Oxyrhynchus Papyrus XI no.1364, ed. Hunt, col. 1 line 6–col. 7 line 15 = 87B44)

17. One's own character inevitably comes to resemble the things
one spends most of one's day with.
(Stobaeus, *Selections* 3.31.41 = 87B62;
tr. Curd, with Reeve and Cohen)

Critias

18. More [people] are good by practice than by nature.
(Stobaeus, *Selections* 3.29.11 = 88B9;
tr. Curd, with Reeve and Cohen)

19. There was a time when human life was without order,
on the level of beasts, and subject to force;
when there was no reward for the good
or punishment for the bad.
And then, I think, humans established
Laws as punishers, so that justice would be the mighty
ruler
of all equally and would have violence as its slave,
and anyone who did wrong would be punished.
(Sextus Empiricus, *Against the Mathematicians*
9.54 = 88B25, lines 1–8)

20. Whoever does everything to please his friends, gives instant
pleasure that later becomes hostility.
(Stobaeus, *Selections* 3.14.2 = 88B27;
tr. Curd, with Reeve and Cohen)

21. It is dreadful when one who is not wise believes himself to
be so.   (Stobaeus, *Selections* 3.14.23 = 88B28;
tr. Curd, with Reeve and Cohen)

22. Wise poverty or stupid wealth—which is the better household
companion?   (Stobaeus, *Selections* 4.33.10 = 88B29;
tr. Curd, with Reeve and Cohen)

23. Nothing is guaranteed, except that what is born will die, and
that in life ruin cannot be avoided.
(pseudo-Dionysus *Art of Rhetoric* 6.2.277.10 = 88B49;
tr. Curd, with Reeve and Cohen)

SUGGESTIONS FOR FURTHER READING

N.B.: Volumes marked with an asterisk (*) are collections of essays. For more complete bibliographies see Barnes, McKirahan, and Mourelatos (1993).

Background and general treatments of the Presocratics:

Barnes, Jonathan, *The Presocratic Philosophers* (London: Routledge and Kegan Paul, 1979; revised edition, 1982).

*Boudouris, K., *Ionian Philosophy* (Athens: International Society for Greek Philosophy, 1989).

Frankfurt, H. et al., *Before Philosophy* (Harmondsworth: Penguin Books, 1949).

Freeman, Kathleen, *Ancilla to the Presocratic Philosophers: A Complete Translation of The Fragments in Diels' Fragmente der Vorsokratiker* (Oxford: Basil Blackwell, 1956).

*Furley, D., *Cosmic Problems* (Cambridge: Cambridge University Press, 1989).

——, *The Greek Cosmologists* (Cambridge, Cambridge University Press, 1987).

*—— and R. E. Allen, eds., *Studies in Presocratic Philosophy* (London: Humanities Press, vol. I, 1970, vol. II, 1975).

Guthrie, W.K.C., *The Greek Philosophers: from Thales to Aristotle* (New York: Harper and Row, 1960; reprint of 1950 Methuen and Co. edition).

——, *A History of Greek Philosophy* (Cambridge: Cambridge University Press, vol. I, 1962, vol. II, 1965, vol. III, 1969).

Hussey, Edward, *The Presocratics* (London: Duckworth, 1972).

Kirk, G. S., J. E. Raven, and M. Schofield, *The Presocratic Philosophers*, second edition (Cambridge: Cambridge University Press, 1983).

*Long, A. A., *The Cambridge Companion to Early Greek Philosophy* (Cambridge: Cambridge University Press, forthcoming).

McKirahan, Richard D., Jr., *Philosophy Before Socrates* (Indianapolis/Cambridge, Mass.: Hackett Publishing, 1994).

*Mourelatos, A.P.D., ed., *The Presocratics* (Princeton: Princeton University Press, 1993); reprint, with updated bibliography, of 1974 Doubleday Anchor edition.

Robinson, John Manley, *An Introduction to Early Greek Philosophy* (Boston: Houghton Mifflin, 1968).

*Shiner, R. A. and J. King-Farlow, *New Essays on Plato and the Presocratics*, *Canadian Journal of Philosophy*, Supplementary Volume 2 (Guelph: 1976).

*Vlastos, G. *Studies in Greek Philosophy* (ed. D. Graham), Vol. I. *The Presocratics* (Princeton: Princeton University Press, 1995).

The Milesians:

Kahn, C. H., *Anaximander and the Origins of Greek Cosmology* (New York: Columbia University Press, 1962; reprinted, Philadelphia: Centrum Philadelphia, 1985; Indianapolis/Cambridge: Hackett, 1994).

Xenophanes:

Lesher, J. H., *Xenophanes of Colophon: Fragments. A Text and Translation with a Commentary* (Toronto: University of Toronto Press, 1992).

Pythagoras and Pythagoreanism:

*Boudouris, K. J., ed., *Pythagorean Philosophy* (Athens: International Society for Greek Philosophy, 1991).

Burkert, W., *Lore and Science in Ancient Pythagoreanism*, tr. E. L. Minar, Jr. (Cambridge, Mass.: Harvard University Press, 1972).

Huffman, C., *Philolaus of Croton: Pythagorean and Presocratic* (Cambridge: Cambridge University Press, 1993).

de Vogel, C. J., *Pythagoras and Early Pythagoreanism* (Assen: Van Gorcum, 1966).

Heraclitus:

*Hospers, J. and K. Robb, eds. *Heraclitus: The Monist* 74, no. 4 (1991).

Kahn, C. H., *The Art and Thought of Heraclitus* (Cambridge: Cambridge University Press, 1979).

Kirk, G. S., *Heraclitus: The Cosmic Fragments*, second edition (Cambridge: Cambridge University Press, 1962).

Robinson, T. M., *Heraclitus: Fragments. A Text and Translation with a Commentary* (Toronto: The University of Toronto Press, 1987).

Parmenides, Zeno, and Melissus:

Cornford, F. M., *Plato and Parmenides* (London: Routledge & Kegan Paul, 1939; reprinted Indianapolis: Bobbs-Merrill, n.d.).

Coxon, A. H., *The Fragments of Parmenides* (Assen: Van Gorcum, 1986).

Curd, P., *The Legacy of Parmenides: Eleatic Monism and Later Presocratic Thought* (Princeton: Princeton University Press, 1997).

Gallop, D., *Parmenides of Elea: Fragments. A Text with an Introduction* (Toronto: University of Toronto Press, 1984).

Grünbaum, A., *Modern Science and Zeno's Paradoxes,* revised edition (London: Allen and Unwin, 1968).

Lee, H.P.D., *Zeno of Elea* (Cambridge: Cambridge University Press, 1936).

Mourelatos, A.P.D., *The Route of Parmenides* (New Haven: Yale University Press, 1971).

*Owens, J., ed., *Parmenides Studies Today: The Monist* 69, no. 1 (1979).

*Salmon, W.C., ed., *Zeno's Paradoxes* (Indianapolis: Bobbs-Merrill, 1970).

Tarán, L., *Parmenides: A Text with Translation, Commentary and Critical Essays* (Princeton: Princeton University Press, 1965).

The Pluralists:

Inwood, B., *The Poem of Empedocles: A Text and Translation with an Introduction* (Toronto: The University of Toronto Press, 1992).

O'Brien, D., *Empedocles' Cosmic Cycle: A Reconstruction from the Fragments and Secondary Sources* (Cambridge: Cambridge University Press, 1969).

Schofield, Malcolm, *An Essay on Anaxagoras* (Cambridge: Cambridge University Press, 1980).

Wright, M. R., *Empedocles: The Extant Fragments* (Indianapolis and Cambridge, Mass.: Hackett Publishing Company, Inc. and London: Gerald Duckworth & Co. Ltd., 1995).

The Atomists:

Furley, *Two Studies in the Greek Atomists* (Princeton: Princeton University Press, 1967).

O'Brien, D., *Theories of Weight in the Ancient World: Four Essays on Democritus, Plato, and Aristotle. A Study in the Development of Ideas, vol. I: Democritus, Weight, and Size: An Exercise in the Reconstruction of Early Greek Philosophy* (Leiden: E. J. Brill, 1981).

The Sophists:

de Romilly, J., *The Great Sophists in Periclean Athens,* tr. J. Lloyd (Oxford: The Clarendon Press, 1992).

Guthrie, W.K.C., *The Sophists* (Cambridge: Cambridge University Press, 1971).

Kerferd, G. B., *The Sophistic Movement* (Cambridge: Cambridge University Press, 1981).

* ——, ed., *The Sophists and Their Legacy* (Wiesbaden: Franz Steiner, 1981).

Sprague, R. K., *The Older Sophists: A Complete Translation by Several Hands* (Columbia, S.C.: University of South Carolina Press, 1972).

CONCORDANCE
AND SOURCES

DK number	APR number (or page)	Source

Alcmaeon
(DK24)

| B1 | p.4 | Diogenes Laertius, *Lives of the Philosophers* 8.83 |

Anaxagoras (Pluralists)
(DK59)

A46	27	Aristotle, *On Generation and Corruption* I.1 314a18–20
A52	25	Aristotle, *Physics* I.4 187a23–b6
B1	1	Simplicius, *Commentary on Aristotle's Physics* 155.26–30
B2	2	Simplicius, *Commentary on Aristotle's Physics* 155.31–156.1
B3	3	Simplicius, *Commentary on Aristotle's Physics* 164.17–20
B4a	4	Simplicius, *Commentary on Aristotle's Physics* 34.29–35.9
B4b	5	Simplicius, *Commentary on Aristotle's Physics* 34.21–26
B5	6	Simplicius, *Commentary on Aristotle's Physics* 156.10–12
B6	7	Simplicius, *Commentary on Aristotle's Physics* 164.26–165.1
B7	8	Simplicius, *Commentary on Aristotle's On the Heavens* 608.26
B8	9	Simplicius, *Commentary on Aristotle's Physics* 175.12–14; 176.29
B9	10	Simplicius, *Commentary on Aristotle's Physics* 35.14–18
B10	11	Scholiast on Gregory of Nazianzus 36.911 Migne

B11	12	Simplicius, *Commentary on Aristotle's Physics* 164.23–24
B12	13	Simplicius, *Commentary on Aristotle's Physics* 164.24–25; 156.13–157.4
B13	14	Simplicius, *Commentary on Aristotle's Physics* 300.31–301.1
B14	15	Simplicius, *Commentary on Aristotle's Physics* 157.7–9
B15	16	Simplicius, *Commentary on Aristotle's Physics* 179.3–6
B16	17	Simplicius, *Commentary on Aristotle's Physics* 179.8–10; 155.21–23
B17	18	Simplicius, *Commentary on Aristotle's Physics* 163.20–24
B18	19	Plutarch, *On the Face in the Moon* 929B
B19	20	Scholium BT on *Iliad* 17.547
B21	21	Sextus Empiricus, *Against the Mathematicians* 7.90
B21a	22	Sextus Empiricus, *Against the Mathematicians* 7.140
B21b	23	Plutarch, *On Fortune* 98F
B22	24	Athenaeus, *Deipnosophists* II 57B

Anaximander (Milesians)
(DK12)

A9	6	Simplicius, *Commentary on Aristotle's Physics* 24.13–21
A10	8, 14	pseudo-Plutarch, *Miscellanies* 179.2
A11	9	Hippolytus, *Refutation of All Heresies* 1.6.3–5
A15	7	Aristotle, *Physics* III.4 203b10–15
A18	12	Aetius 2.16.5
A21	11	Aetius 2.21.1
A26	10	Aristotle, *On the Heavens* II.13 295b11–16
A30	13, 15	Aetius 5.19.4, Censorinus, *On the Day of Birth* 4.7
B1	6	Simplicius, *Commentary on Aristotle's Physics* 24.13–21

Anaximenes (Milesians)
(DK13)

A5	16	Theophrastus, quoted in Simplicius, *Commentary on Aristotle's Physics* 24.26–25.1
A6	22	pseudo-Plutarch, *Miscellanies* 3
A7	18, 24	Hippolytus, *Refutation of All Heresies* 1.7.1–3; 1.7.4

A10	19	Cicero, *On the Nature of the Gods* 1.10.26
A17	20	Aetius 3.4.1
A20	23	Aristotle, *On the Heavens* II.13 294b13–20
B1	21	Plutarch, *The Principle of Cold* 7.947F
B2	17	Aetius 1.3.4

Antiphon (Sophists)
(DK87)

B1	11	Galen, *Commentary on Hippocrates' The Doctor's Workshop* 18B656
B2	12	Galen, *Commentary on Hippocrates' The Doctor's Workshop* 18B656
B9	13	Aetius 1.22.6
B10	14	Suda *v. adeētos*
B15	15	Harpocration, *Lexicon v. embios*
B44	16	Oxyrhynchus Papyrus XI no. 1364 ed. Hunt, col. 1 line 6–col. 7 line 15
B62	17	Stobaeus, *Selections* 3.31.41

Aristotle

On the Heavens III.3 302a28–b3 Anaxagoras 26
Physics VIII.8 263a15–18 Zeno 9

Critias (Sophists)
(DK88)

B9	18	Stobaeus, *Selections* 3.29.11
B25	19	Sextus Empiricus, *Against the Mathematicians* 9.54
B27	20	Stobaeus, *Selections* 3.14.2
B28	21	Stobaeus, *Selections* 3.14.23
B29	22	Stobaeus, *Selections* 4.33.10
B49	23	pseudo-Dionysius, *Art of Rhetoric* 6.2.277.10

Democritus (Atomism)
(DK68)

A37	5	Aristotle, *On Democritus*, quoted in Simplicius, *Commentary on Aristotle's On the Heavens* 295.1–22
A38	6	Simplicius, *Commentary on Aristotle's Physics* 28.4–26
A47	9, 18	Aetius 1.3.18; Simplicius, *Commentary on Aristotle's Physics* 42.10–11; Aetius 1.12.6; 1.23.3

A48b	12	Aristotle, *On Generation and Corruption* I.2 316a–b16
A57	19	Plutarch, *Against Colotes* 1110F-1111A
A59	8	Sextus Empiricus, *Against the Mathematicians* 8.6
A66	2	Aristotle, *Generation of Animals* V.8 789b2–4; Aetius 1.26.2
A129	20	Theophrastus, *Causes of Plants* 6.1.6
B6	23	Sextus Empiricus, *Against the Mathematicians* 7.136
B8	24	Sextus Empiricus, *Against the Mathematicians* 7.136
B7	25	Sextus Empiricus, *Against the Mathematicians* 7.136
B9	21, 26	Sextus Empiricus, *Against the Mathematicians* 7.136; 135
B11	22	Sextus Empiricus, *Against the Mathematicians* 7.138
B69	30	Democrates, *Maxims*
B74	29	Democrates, *Maxims*
B125	27	Galen, *On Medical Experience* 15.8
B156	14	Plutarch, *Against Colotes* 1108F
B189	31	Stobaeus, *Selections* 3.1.147
B191	28	Stobaeus, *Selections* 1.210
B235	32	Stobaeus, *Selections* 3.18.35

Diogenes of Apollonia
(DK64)

A1	8	Diogenes Laertius, *Lives of the Philosophers* 9.57
A6	9	pseudo-Plutarch, *Miscellanies* 12 = 64A6
A19	10	Theophrastus, *On the Senses* 39–45
B1	1	Diogenes Laertius, *Lives of the Philosophers* 9.57
B2	2	Simplicius, *Commentary on Aristotle's Physics* 151.31–152.7
B3	3	Simplicius, *Commentary on Aristotle's Physics* 152.12–16
B4	4	Simplicius, *Commentary on Aristotle's Physics* 152.18–21
B5	5	Simplicius, *Commentary on Aristotle's Physics* 152.22–153.17
B7	6	Simplicius, *Commentary on Aristotle's Physics* 153.19–20
B8	7	Simplicius, *Commentary on Aristotle's Physics* 153.20–22

Empedocles (Pluralists)
(DK31)

B2	59	Sextus Empiricus, *Against the Mathematicians* 7.123
B6	33	Aetius 1.3.20
B8	45	Plutarch, *Against Colotes* 1111F
B9	46	Plutarch, *Against Colotes* 1113D
B11	43	Plutarch, *Against Colotes* 1113C
B12	44	[Aristotle] *On Melissus Xenophanes Gorgias* 2 975b1–4
B13	47	Aetius 1.18.2
B16	35	Hippolytus, *Refutation of All Heresies* 7.29.9
B17	32	Simplicius, *Commentary on Aristotle's Physics* 158.1–159.4
B21	34	Simplicius, *Commentary on Aristotle's Physics* 159.13–26
B23	36	Simplicius, *Commentary on Aristotle's Physics* 160.1–11
B26	50	Simplicius, *Commentary on Aristotle's Physics* 33.19–34.3
B28	51	Stobaeus, *Selections* 1.15.2
B35	48	Simplicius, *Commentary on Aristotle's On the Heavens* 529.1–15 (lines 1–51); *Commentary on Aristotle's Physics* 32.13–33.2 (lines 3–17)
B36	49	Stobaeus, *Selections* 1.10.11
B38	30	Clement, *Miscellanies* 5.48.3
B57	52	Simplicius, *Commentary on Aristotle's On the Heavens* 586.12; 587.1–2
B58	53	Simplicius, *Commentary on Aristotle's On the Heavens* 587.18–19
B59	54	Simplicius, *Commentary on Aristotle's On the Heavens* 587.20; 23
B61	55	Aelian, *The Nature of Animals* 16.29
B73	37	Simplicius, *Commentary on Aristotle's On the Heavens* 530.6–7
B75	38	Simplicius, *Commentary on Aristotle's On the Heavens* 530.9–10
B84	57	Aristotle, *On the Senses and Their Objects* 2 437b24–438a5
B91	39	Philoponus, *Commentary on Aristotle's Generation of Animals* 123.19–20
B92	40	Aristotle, *Generation of Animals* 2.8 747a34–b6

B96	41	Simplicius, *Commentary on Aristotle's Physics* 300.21–24
B98	42	Simplicius, *Commentary on Aristotle's Physics* 32.6–10
B105	58	Porphyry, quoted in Stobaeus, *Selections* 1.49.53
B109	56	Aristotle, *On the Soul* 1.2 404b11–15
B110	29	Hippolytus, *Refutation of All Heresies* 7.29.25
B112	28	lines 1–10: Diogenes Laertius, *Lives of the Philosophers* 8.62; lines 9–11: Clement, *Miscellanies* 6.30
B115	61	Hippolytus, *Refutation of All Heresies* 7.29.14–23 (lines 1–2, 4–14); Plutarch, *On Exile* 607C (lines 1, 3, 5–16, 13)
B129	Pyth. 5	Porphyry, *Life of Pythagoras* 30
B132	60	Clement, *Miscellanies* 5.140.5
B133	31	Clement, *Miscellanies* 5.81.2
B135	62	Aristotle, *Rhetoric* I 1373b16–17
B136	63	Sextus Empiricus, *Against the Mathematicians* 9.129
B137	64	Sextus Empiricus, *Against the Mathematicians* 9.129
B144	65	Plutarch, *The Control of Anger* 464B

Gorgias (Sophists) (DK82)

B3	6	Sextus Empiricus, *Against the Mathematicians* 7.65–86
B11	7	*Encomium of Helen*
B12	8	Aristotle, *Rhetoric* III.18 1419b3
B23	9	Plutarch, *On the Fame of the Athenians* 5.348C
B29	10	*Gnomologium Vaticanum* 743 no. 166

Heraclitus (DK22)

B1	1	Sextus Empiricus, *Against the Mathematicians* 7.132
B2	2	Sextus Empiricus, *Against the Mathematicians* 7.133
B3	89	Aetius 2.21
B4	53	Albertus Magnus, *On Vegetables* 6.401
B5	91	Aristocritus, *Theosophia* 68; Origen, *Against Celsus* 7.62
B6	88	Aristotle, *Meteorology* II.2 355a13

B7	34	Aristotle, *On the Senses and Their Objects* 5 443a23
B8	49	Aristotle, *Nicomachean Ethics* VIII.2 1155b4
B9	52	Aristotle, *Nicomachean Ethics* X.5 1176a7
B10	45	[Aristotle] *On the World* 5 396b20
B11	13	[Aristotle] *On the World* 6 401a10
B12	61	Arius Didymus, Fr. 39.2 (*Dox. Gr.* 471.4-5)
B13b	51	Clement, *Miscellanies* 1.2.2
B14	93	Clement, *Protreptic* 22.2
B15	92	Clement, *Protreptic* 34.5
B16	102	Clement, *Pedagogue* 2.99.5
B17	3	Clement, *Miscellanies* 2.8.1
B18	36	Clement, *Miscellanies* 2.17.4
B19	18	Clement, *Miscellanies* 2.24.5
B21	24	Clement, *Miscellanies* 3.21.1
B22	37	Clement, *Miscellanies* 4.4.2
B23	69	Clement, *Miscellanies* 4.9.7
B24	98	Clement, *Miscellanies* 4.16.1
B25	99	Clement, *Miscellanies* 4.49.2
B26	23	Clement, *Miscellanies* 4.141.2
B27	100	Clement, *Miscellanies* 4.22.144
B28	17	Clement, *Miscellanies* 5.9.3
B29	4	Clement, *Miscellanies* 5.59.4
B30	74	Clement, *Miscellanies* 5.103.6
B31a, b	72	Clement, *Miscellanies* 5.104.3, 5
B32	27	Clement, *Miscellanies* 5.115.1
B33	84	Clement, *Miscellanies* 5.155.2
B34	20	Clement, *Miscellanies* 5.115.3
B35	31	Clement, *Miscellanies* 5.140.5
B36	71	Clement, *Miscellanies* 6.17.2
B37	54	Columella, *On Agriculture* 8.4.4
B40	14; Pyth. 2	Diogenes Laertius, *Lives of the Philosophers* 9.1
B41	41	Diogenes Laertius, *Lives of the Philosophers* 9.1
B42	16	Diogenes Laertius, *Lives of the Philosophers* 9.1
B43	111	Diogenes Laertius, *Lives of the Philosophers* 9.1
B44	110	Diogenes Laertius, *Lives of the Philosophers* 9.2
B45	104	Diogenes Laertius, *Lives of the Philosophers* 9.7
B47	42	Diogenes Laertius, *Lives of the Philosophers* 9.73
B48	65	*Etymologicum Magnum* sv bios
B49	108	Theodorus Prodromus, *Letters* 1
B49a	63	Heraclitus, *Homeric Questions* 24 Oelmann (Schleiermacher fr. 72)
B50	44	Hippolytus, *Refutation of All Heresies* 9.9.1

B51	46	Hippolytus, *Refutation of All Heresies* 9.9.2
B52	109	Hippolytus, *Refutation of All Heresies* 9.9.4
B53	79	Hippolytus, *Refutation of All Heresies* 9.9.4
B54	47	Hippolytus, *Refutation of All Heresies* 9.9.5
B55	32	Hippolytus, *Refutation of All Heresies* 9.9.5
B56	5	Hippolytus, *Refutation of All Heresies* 9.9.5
B57	68	Hippolytus, *Refutation of All Heresies* 9.10.2
B58	58	Hippolytus, *Refutation of All Heresies* 9.10.3
B59	59	Hippolytus, *Refutation of All Heresies* 9.10.4
B60	60	Hippolytus, *Refutation of All Heresies* 9.10.4
B61	50	Hippolytus, *Refutation of All Heresies* 9.10.5
B62	86	Hippolytus, *Refutation of All Heresies* 9.10.6
B63	101	Hippolytus, *Refutation of All Heresies* 9.10.6
B64	78	Hippolytus, *Refutation of All Heresies* 9.10.7
B65	82	Hippolytus, *Refutation of All Heresies* 9.10.7
B66	81	Hippolytus, *Refutation of All Heresies* 9.10.6
B67	83	Hippolytus, *Refutation of All Heresies* 9.10.8
B70	6	Stobaeus, *Selections* 2.1.16
B72	7	Marcus Aurelius, *Meditations* 4.46
B73	21	Marcus Aurelius, *Meditations* 4.46
B76a	73	Maximus of Tyre 41.4
B77	95	Numenius, fr. 30 quoted in Porphyry, *The Cave of the Nymphs* 10
B78	25	Origen, *Against Celsus* 6.12
B79	26	Origen, *Against Celsus* 6.12
B80	80	Origen, *Against Celsus* 6.42
B82	55	Plato, *Hippias Major* 289a3–4
B83	56	Plato, *Hippias Major* 289b4–5
B84a	75	Plotinus, *Enneads* 4.8.1
B84b	38	Plotinus, *Enneads* 4.8.1
B85	115	Plutarch, *Coriolanus* 22.2
B86	8	Plutarch, *Coriolanus* 38; Clement, *Miscellanies* 5.88.4
B87	9	Plutarch, *On Listening to Lectures* 40F–41A
B88	67	pseudo-Plutarch, *Consolation to Apollonius* 106E
B89	22	pseudo-Plutarch, *On Superstition* 166C
B90	77	Plutarch, *On the E at Delphi* 338D-E
B91a, b	62	Plutarch, *On the E at Delphi* 392B
B92	94	Plutarch, *Why the Pythia No Longer Prophesies in Verse* 397A
B93	40	Plutarch, *On the Pythian Oracle* 404D
B94	87	Plutarch, *On Exile* 604a
B95	114	Plutarch, *Table Talk* 644F

B96	103	Plutarch, *Table Talk* 669A
B97	10	Plutarch, *Should Old Men Take Part in Politics?* 787C
B98	35	Plutarch, *On the Face in the Moon* 943E
B99	90	Plutarch, *Is Water or Fire the More Useful?* 957A
B101	30	Plutarch, *Against Colotes* 1118C
B101a	33	Polybius, *Histories* 12.27.1
B102	85	Porphyry, *Notes on Homer*, on *Iliad* 4.4
B103	64	Porphyry, *Notes on Homer*, on *Iliad* 24.200
B104	11	Proclus, *Commentary on Plato's Alcibiades I*, p. 117, Westerink
B107	19	Sextus Empiricus, *Against the Mathematicians* 7.126
B108	12	Stobaeus, *Selections* 3.1.174
B110	113	Stobaeus, *Selections* 3.1.176
B111	70	Stobaeus, *Selections* 3.1.178
B112	43	Stobaeus, *Selections* 3.1.178
B113	28	Stobaeus, *Selections* 3.1.179
B114	48	Stobaeus, *Selections* 3.1.179
B115	105	Stobaeus, *Selections* 3.1.180
B116	29	Stobaeus, *Selections* 3.5.6
B117	97	Stobaeus, *Selections* 3.5.7
B118	96	Stobaeus, *Selections* 3.5.8
B119	112	Stobaeus, *Selections* 4.40.23
B121	106	Strabo 14.25
B123	39	Themistius, *Orations* 5.69b
B124	57	Theophrastus, *Metaphysics* 15 (p. 16 Ross and Fobes)
B125	76	Theophrastus, *On Vertigo* 9
B125a	107	John Tzetzes, Scholium on Aristophanes' *Plutus* 88
B126	66	John Tzetzes, *Notes on the Iliad* p. 126 Hermann
B129	15; Pyth. 3	Diogenes Laertius, *Lives of the Philosophers* 8.6

Hesiod

Theogony 114–139, pp. 2–3

Hippasos
(DK18)

2	Pyth. 8	Iamblichus, *Life of Pythagoras* 81, 82

Homer

Iliad 2.484–92, pp. 4–5

Ion
(DK36)

B4   Pyth. 4   Diogenes Laertius, *Lives of the Philosophers* 1.120

Leucippus (Atomism)
(DK67)

A6   3   Aristotle, *Metaphysics* I.4 985b4–20
A7   13   Philoponus, *Commentary on Aristotle's On the Heavens* 158.27–159.3
A8   6   Simplicius, *Commentary on Aristotle's Physics* 28.4–26
A13   11   Simplicius, *Commentary on Aristotle's Physics* 925.10–15
A14   10   Simplicius, *Commentary on Aristotle's On the Heavens* 242.18–26
A16   17   Simplicius, *Commentary on Aristotle's On the Heavens* 583.18–20
A18   16   Aristotle, *Metaphysics* XII.6 1071b33–35
A19   7, 15   Aristotle, *On the Heavens* I.7 275b32–276a1; *Physics* IV.6 213a27–b22
A97   4   Aristotle, *On Generation and Corruption* I.1 315b6–15
B2   1   Aetius 1.25.4

Melissus
(DK30)

A5   11   [Aristotle] *On Melissus Xenophanes Gorgias* I 974a12–14
B1   1   Simplicius, *Commentary on Aristotle's Physics* 162.23–26
B2   2   Simplicius, *Commentary on Aristotle's Physics* 29.22–26; 109.20–25
B3   3   Simplicius, *Commentary on Aristotle's Physics* 109.29–32
B4   4   Simplicius, *Commentary on Aristotle's Physics* 110.2–4
B5   5   Simplicius, *Commentary on Aristotle's Physics* 110.5–6
B6   6   Simplicius, *Commentary on Aristotle's On the Heavens* 557.14–17
B7   7   Simplicius, *Commentary on Aristotle's Physics* 111.18–112.15

B8	8	Simplicius, *Commentary on Aristotle's On the Heavens* 558.19–559.12
B9	9	Simplicius, *Commentary on Aristotle's Physics* 109.34–110.2
B10	10	Simplicius, *Commentary on Aristotle's Physics* 109.32–34

Parmenides
(DK28)

B1	1	lines 1–30: Sextus Empiricus, *Against the Mathematicians* 7.111–14; lines 28–32: Simplicius, *Commentary on Aristotle's On the Heavens* 557.25–558.2
B2	2	Proclus, *Commentary on Plato's Timaeus* 1.345.18; lines 3–8: Simplicius, *Commentary on Aristotle's Physics* 116.28–117.1
B3	3	Clement, *Miscellanies* 6.23; Plotinus, *Enneads* 5.1.8
B4	4	Clement, *Miscellanies* 5.15.5
B5	5	Proclus, *Commentary on Plato's Parmenides* 1.708 (16 Cousin)
B6	6	Simplicius, *Commentary on Aristotle's Physics* 86.27–8; 117.4–13
B7	7	lines 1–2: Plato, *Sophist* 237a8–9; lines 2–6: Sextus Empiricus, *Against the Mathematicians* 7.114
B8	8	Simplicius, *Commentary on Aristotle's Physics* 145.1–146.25 (lines 1–52); 39.1–9 (lines 50–61)
B9	9	Simplicius, *Commentary on Aristotle's Physics* 180.9–12
B10	10	Clement, *Miscellanies* 5.14, 138.1
B11	11	Simplicius, *Commentary on Aristotle's On the Heavens* 559.22–25
B12	12	Simplicius, *Commentary on Aristotle's Physics* 39.14–16 (lines 1–3); 31.13–17 (lines 2–6)
B13	13	Simplicius, *Commentary on Aristotle's Physics* 39.18
B14	14	Plutarch, *Against Colotes* 1116A
B15	15	Plutarch, *On the Face in the Moon* 929AB
B16	16	Theophrastus, *On the Senses* 3
B17	17	Galen, *Commentary on Book VI of Hippocrates' Epidemics* II.46
B19	18	Simplicius, *Commentary on Aristotle's On the Heavens* 558.9–11
"The Cornford Fragment"	19	Plato, *Theaetetus* 180e1

Philolaus (Pythagoreanism)
(DK44)

B1	17	Diogenes Laertius, *Lives of the Philosophers* 8.85
B2	18	Stobaeus, *Selections* 1.21.7a
B4	21	Stobaeus, *Selections* 1.21.7b
B5	22	Stobaeus, *Selections* 1.21.7c
B6	19	Stobaeus, *Selections* 1.21.7d
B6a	20	Stobaeus, *Selections* 1.21.7d
B7	23	Stobaeus, *Selections* 1.21.8

Protagoras (Sophists)
(DK80)

B1	1	Sextus Empiricus, *Against the Mathematicians* 7.60
B4	2	Eusebius, *Preparation of the Gospel* 14.3.7
B6a	3	Diogenes Laertius, *Lives of the Philosophers* 9.51
B6b	4	Aristotle, *Rhetoric* II.24 1402a23
B11	5	Plutarch, *On Practice* 178.25

Pythagoras
(DK14)

2	8	Iamblichus, *Life of Pythagoras* 81, 82
8	7	Diogenes Laertius, *Lives of the Philosophers* 8.4–5
8a	6	Porphyry, *Life of Pythagoras* 19

Pythagorean School
(DK58)

B4	11, 16	Aristotle, *Metaphysics* I.5 985b23–986a2; 986a1–2
B5	12	Aristotle, *Metaphysics* I.5 986a17–21
B8	13	Aristotle, *Metaphysics* I.5 987a13–19
B28	14	Aristotle, *Physics* III.4 203a10–15
C3	10	Aristotle fr. 195 [Rose], in Diogenes Laertius, *Lives of the Philosophers* 8.34–35
C4	8, 9	Iamblichus, *Life of Pythagoras* 81, 82

Sextus Empiricus
Against the Mathematicians 7.94–95   Pythagoras 15

Thales (Milesians)
(DK11)

A2	1	Aristotle, *Metaphysics* I.3 983b6–18
A9	p. 8	Plato, *Theaetetus* 174a4–8
A10	p. 8	Aristotle, *Politics* I.11 1259a9–18
A12	2, p. 12	Aristotle, *Metaphysics* I.3 983b18–27; 22–27
A14	3	Aristotle, *On the Heavens* II.13 294a28–34
A22	4, 5	Aristotle, *On the Soul* I.5 411a7–8; 1.2 405a19–21

Xenophanes
(DK21)

A12	7	Aristotle, *Rhetoric* II.23 1399b6–9
A33	18	Hippolytus, *Refutation of All Heresies* 1.14.5–6
A39	16	Aetius 2.18.1
B7	Pyth. 1	Diogenes Laertius, *Lives of the Philosophers* 8.36
B8	1	Diogenes Laertius, *Lives of the Philosophers* 9.18
B1	2	Athenaeus, *Scholars at Dinner* 11.462c
(21–24)		
B11	3	Sextus Empiricus, *Against the Mathematicians* 9.193
B14	4	Clement, *Miscellanies* 5.109
B15	6	Clement, *Miscellanies* 5.110
B16	5	Clement, *Miscellanies* 7.22
B18	12	Stobaeus, *Selections* 1.8.2
B23	8	Clement, *Miscellanies* 5.109
B24	9	Sextus Empiricus, *Against the Mathematicians* 9.144
B25	10	Simplicius, *Commentary on Aristotle's Physics* 23.19
B26	11	Simplicius, *Commentary on Aristotle's Physics* 23.10
B29	19	Philoponus, *Commentary on Aristotle's Physics* 125.30
B30	17	Geneva Scholium on *Iliad* 21.196
B32	15	Scholium BLT on *Iliad* 11.27
B34	13	Sextus Empiricus, *Against the Mathematicians* 7.49.110
B35	14	Plutarch, *Table Talk* 9.7.746B
B38	20	Herodian, *On Peculiar Speech* 41.5

Zeno of Elea
(DK29)

A11	1	Plato, the *Parmenides* 127b
A12	1	Plato, the *Parmenides* 128b-d
A16	2	Eudemus, *Physics* fr. 7 quoted in Simplicius, *Commentary on Aristotle's Physics* 97.12–13
A24	12	Aristotle, *Physics* IV.3 210b22–23; IV.1 209a23–25; Eudemus *Physics* fr. 42 quoted in Simplicius, *Commentary on Aristotle's Physics* 563.25–28
A25	6, 8	Aristotle, *Physics* VI.9 239b9–13; 6.2.233a21–31
A26	7	Aristotle, *Physics* VI.9 239b14–20
A27	10	Aristotle, *Physics* VI.9 239b5–7; b30–33
A28	11	Aristotle, *Physics* VI.9 239b33–240a17

A29	13	Simplicius, *Commentary on Aristotle's Physics* 1108.18–25
B1	4	Simplicius, *Commentary on Aristotle's Physics* 141.2–8
B2	3	Simplicius, *Commentary on Aristotle's Physics* 139.11–15
B3	5	Simplicius, *Commentary on Aristotle's Physics* 140.29–33
B5	12	Simplicius, *Commentary on Aristotle's Physics* 562.3–6